The Law
(In Plain English)®
for
Doctors, Dentists, and Other Health Professionals

Leonard D. DuBoff, Esq.

Christy O. King, Esq.

Professor Michael D. Murray

SPHINX® PUBLISHING
AN IMPRINT OF SOURCEBOOKS, INC.®
NAPERVILLE, ILLINOIS
www.SphinxLegal.com

First Edition: 2008

Published by: **Sphinx® Publishing, An Imprint of Sourcebooks, Inc.®**

<u>Naperville Office</u>
P.O. Box 4410
Naperville, Illinois 60567-4410
630-961-3900
Fax: 630-961-2168
www.sourcebooks.com
www.SphinxLegal.com

This publication is designed to provide accurate and authoritative information in regard to the subject matter covered. It is sold with the understanding that the publisher is not engaged in rendering legal, accounting, or other professional service. If legal advice or other expert assistance is required, the services of a competent professional person should be sought.

From a Declaration of Principles Jointly Adopted by a Committee of the
American Bar Association and a Committee of Publishers and Associations

This product is not a substitute for legal advice.

Disclaimer required by Texas statutes.

Library of Congress Cataloging-in-Publication Data
DuBoff, Leonard D.
  Law (in plain English) for doctors, dentists, and other health professionals / by Leonard D. DuBoff and Christy King, and Michael Murray. -- 1st ed.
      p. cm.
  Includes index.
  ISBN 978-1-57248-615-7 (pbk. : alk. paper) 1. Law--United States. 2. Medical care--Law and legislation--United States. 3. Physicians--United States--Handbooks, manuals, etc. 4. Dentists--United States--Handbooks, manuals, etc. I. King, Christy O., 1969- II. Murray, Michael D., 1965- III. Title.
  KF390.P45D829 2008
  349.73--dc22
                    2008017287

Printed and bound in the United States of America.
SB 10 9 8 7 6 5 4 3 2 1

Contents

Content Requirements
HIPAA
Length of Retention of Records
Special Confidentiality Statutes and Considerations
Necessity of Consent

Business Records and Accounting
Business Year
Cash and Accrual Bookkeeping Methods
Current and Capital Expenditures
Financial Statements
Intangible Business Characteristics
Sources of Information on Accounting

Income Spreading
Installments
Deferred Payments
Spreading Income Among Family Members
Tax Advantages and Disadvantages of Incorporation
S Corporations
LLC Tax Election
Taxes on Accumulated Earnings and Passive Investment Income
Qualifying for Business Deductions
Charitable Deductions
Grants, Prizes, and Awards
Health Insurance

Defined Benefit Plans
Defined Contribution Plans
Profit-Sharing Plans

Acknowledgments

The task of updating this book could not have been undertaken without the support and assistance of numerous individuals. While it would be impossible to identify all of them, there are some who deserve special recognition. We would, therefore, like to thank our friends and colleagues for all their help and, in particular, Jed C. Macy, a pension consultant at The Macy Company; Christopher Johnson, an accountant with a prominent Portland firm; Professor Sherri L. Burr of the University of New Mexico School of Law; Professor Richard Kaplan of the University of Illinois College of Law; Mary Ann DuBoff, a paralegal at The DuBoff Law Group; and Peggy Reckow, a legal assistant at The DuBoff Law Group.

We would also like to thank Michael Bowen, the senior legal editor at Sourcebooks, Inc., for his help in arranging the publication of this work; and Erin R. Shanahan, the managing editor of Sphinx Publishing, an imprint of Sourcebooks, Inc., for her support, insight, and confidence with respect to this project.

Leonard D. DuBoff
Christy O. King
Michael D. Murray
2008

Introduction to the New Edition

It has been almost two decades since *The Law (In Plain English)® for Health Care Professionals* was first written. Since that time, both the legislatures and courts have been extremely active, resulting in significant changes in the law. As a result, it has become necessary to revise and update the original text.

In order to accomplish this task, my colleague, attorney Christy King of The DuBoff Law Group, LLC, and Professor Michael Murray of the University of Illinois College of Law have collaborated with me in preparing this edition. As with the first edition, the primary purpose of the text is to provide health care professionals with the tools necessary to work with their attorneys in connection with creating and building their practices.

In this edition, we have also provided a glossary of legal terms so that you will have the necessary vocabulary to effectively communicate with your lawyer on a regular basis.

We have also highlighted specific areas where we feel that it is particularly important to be diligent in order to be as proactive as possible in protecting your practice and, hopefully, to avoid costly litigation.

We sincerely hope that, as with the other books in *The Law (In Plain English)®* series, this volume will be useful, readable, and understandable so that you can work as efficiently as possible with your professional legal advisor.

Leonard DuBoff
Portland, Oregon
2008

Introduction to the Original Edition

For some time, friends, relatives, and clients who are medical professionals made it clear to me that there was a need for a book that would aid them in understanding the myriad business problems they encounter on a regular basis. All felt confident with respect to their medical skills, but when it came to structuring their profession as a business, they felt somewhat insecure. Professional schools rarely provide the kind of education that will enable a graduate to properly structure a practice so as to achieve the maximum protection afforded by the law while deriving the maximum business benefits possible.

While professionals, such as lawyers and accountants, are available to assist a medical or dental practitioner with the complex business, tax, and other legal issues that arise in practice, it is still not always clear when help is needed until a situation has so deteriorated as to be irretrievable. In addition, if one takes certain precautions and is careful to provide the proper foundation for necessary business transactions, many difficulties can be avoided.

As a law professor for more than two decades, I have learned the importance of preproblem counseling. I have advised my students that it is important for them to service their clients by using all possible methods of avoiding costly and time-consuming litigation. Unfortunately, our legal system is quite complex and is constantly changing. It is often quite difficult to identify potential legal problems and to avoid becoming entangled in litigation.

The purpose of this text is to provide licensed medical and dental professionals with a single readable volume that will assist them in identifying most of the legal issues they will have to evaluate and deal with in their practice. The primary focus of this book is on the business of being a licensed medical or dental professional. Each of the subjects considered could actually support a multivolume treatise as well as a law school course. Many do, and therefore, the treatment here is quite general. We hope that you will use this book to sensitize yourself to the variety of issues to be discussed with your attorney, accountant, or other business advisor.

While there is a chapter devoted to professional liability, this is not the primary focus of this book. It is included because it is one of the many issues encountered by medical and dental practitioners, and any book that purports to serve as a business counseling tool would be incomplete without such a discussion. Most professional associations have books, pamphlets, and videos aimed more directly at professional liability, and it is essential for you to continue to update your knowledge regarding the problems that can and do arise in your specialty.

CHAPTER 1

Organizing Your Business

Everyone in business—and all professionals are engaged in business—knows that survival requires careful financial planning, yet few fully realize the importance of selecting the best legal form for the business. Small health care practices have little need for the sophisticated organizational structures utilized in large, publicly traded corporations, but since all health care professionals must pay taxes, obtain loans, and expose themselves to potential liability, it only makes sense to structure a practice so as to address these issues.

Every business has an organizational form best suited to it. When we counsel people on organizing their businesses, we usually adopt a two-step approach. First, we discuss various aspects of taxation and liability in order to decide which of the basic legal structures is best. Forms that may be available for doctors, dentists, and other health care professionals are the sole proprietorship, the partnership, the corporation, the limited liability company, the limited liability partnership, and a few hybrids. Once we have decided which of these is most appropriate, we draft the organizational documents, such as partnership agreements, corporate bylaws, or operating agreements. These documents define the day-to-day operations of a business and must be tailored to individual situations.

What we offer here is an explanation of the features of each of these kinds of organizations, including their advantages and disadvantages. This should give you an idea of which form might be best for your health care practice, though it should be noted that in many states there are limitations on the organizational forms available to health care and other professionals. We will discuss potential problems, but since we cannot go into a full discussion of the more intricate details, you should consult an experienced business attorney before deciding to adopt any particular structure. Our purpose is to facilitate your communication with your lawyer and enable you to better understand your options.

SOLE PROPRIETORSHIPS

The technical name *sole proprietorship* may be unfamiliar to you, but the notion of a country doctor working in a home office is a classic example. A *sole proprietorship* is an unincorporated business owned by one person. Legal requirements are few and simple. A business license and registration of the name of the practice, if you operate it under a name other than your own, are generally all you need. In addition, you must, of course, have a license to practice your chosen profession, and your profession must permit you to act in your professional capacity independently. With these details taken care of, you are in business.

Disadvantages

There are many financial risks involved in operating your practice as a sole proprietor. If you recognize any of these dangers as a real threat, you probably should consider an alternative form of organization.

If you are the sole proprietor of a health care business venture, all your personal assets are at risk for payment of the practice's debts. In other words, if for any reason you owe more than the dollar value of your practice, your creditors can force the sale of most of your personally owned property to satisfy the debt.

For many risks, insurance is available that shifts the risk of loss from you to an insurance company, but there are some risks for which insurance simply is not available. For instance, insurance is generally not available to protect against a large rise in the cost of or sudden unavailability of medical supplies, pharmaceuticals, or other materials used in your practice. Some types of insurance may be prohibitively expensive. Further, even when procured, every insurance policy has a limited, strictly defined scope of coverage. These liability risks, as well as many other uncertain economic factors, can drive a small health care practice and its sole proprietor into bankruptcy.

Taxes

The sole proprietor is personally taxed on all of the business's profits and may deduct losses. Of course, the rate of taxation will change with increases in income. Fortunately, there are ways to ease this tax burden.

IN PLAIN ENGLISH

Maximize your tax savings by establishing an approved individual retirement account (IRA) or contributing to a pension fund. You can deduct a specified amount of your net income for placement into an interest-bearing account, approved government securities, mutual funds, or company pension plan, and withdraw those funds at a later date—when you are in a lower tax bracket. There may, however, be severe restrictions if you withdraw the money prior to retirement age. (See Chapter 15, "Retirement Plans," for a more complete discussion of this subject.)

For further information on tax planning devices, consult the Internal Revenue Service (IRS) website at **www.irs.gov**, contact your local IRS office and ask for free pamphlets, or use the services of an accountant experienced in business tax planning.

PARTNERSHIPS AND JOINT VENTURES

A *partnership* is defined by most state laws as an association of two or more persons to conduct, as co-owners, a business for profit. No formalities are required. In fact, in some cases, people have been held to be partners even though they never had any intention of forming a partnership. (See "What You Do Not Want: Unintended Partners.")

A *joint venture* is a partnership for a limited or specific purpose, rather than one that continues for an indefinite or specified time. For example, an arrangement whereby two dentists agree to conduct a workshop about treating gingivitis is a joint venture. An agreement to conduct numerous workshops over a period of time is a partnership.

Advantages and Disadvantages

The economic advantages of doing business in a partnership form are:

- the pooling of capital;

- the collaboration of skills;

- easier access to credit enhanced by the collective credit rating; and,

- a potentially more efficient allocation of labor and resources.

A major disadvantage is that each partner is fully and personally liable for all the debts of the partnership, even if not personally involved in incurring those debts. This means each partner is liable for the negligence of another partner and of the partnership's employees when a negligent act occurs in the usual course of business.

If you are getting involved in a partnership, you should be especially cautious in two areas. First, since the involvement of a partner increases your potential liability, you should choose a responsible partner. Second, the partnership should be adequately insured to protect both the assets of the partnership and the personal assets of each partner.

Formalities

No formalities are required to create a partnership. If the partners do not have a formal agreement defining the terms of the partnership—such as control of the partnership or the distribution of profits—state law dictates the terms. State laws are based on the fundamental characteristics of the typical partnership and attempt to correspond to the reasonable expectations of the partners. The most important of these legally presumed characteristics are as follows.

- No one can become an actual member of a partnership without the unanimous consent of all partners.

- Each member has an equal vote in the management of the partnership regardless of the partner's percentage interest in it.

- All partners share equally in the profits and losses of the partnership, no matter how much capital each has contributed.

- A simple majority vote is required for decisions in the ordinary course of business, and a unanimous vote is required to change the fundamental character of the business.

- A partnership is terminable at will by any partner. A partner can withdraw from the partnership at any time, and this withdrawal will cause a dissolution of the partnership.

Most state laws contain a provision that allows the partners to make their own agreements regarding the management structure and division of profits that best suit the needs of the individual partners.

Partnership Agreements

A comprehensive *partnership agreement* is no simple matter. Some major considerations in preparing a partnership agreement include the name of the partnership, a description of the business, contributions of capital by the partners, the duration of the partnership, the distribution of profits, management responsibilities, the duties of partners, prohibited acts, and provisions for the dissolution of the partnership.

(These items are detailed in the next chapter.) It is essential for potential partners to devote time and considerable care to the preparation of this agreement.

IN PLAIN ENGLISH

Enlist the services of a competent business lawyer. The expense of a lawyer to help you put together an agreement suited to the needs of your practice is usually well justified by the economic savings recouped in the smooth organization, operation, and, when necessary, final dissolution of the partnership.

Taxes

A partnership does not possess any special tax advantages over a sole proprietorship. Each partner pays tax on his or her share of the profits, whether distributed or retained, and each is entitled to the same proportion of the partnership deductions and credits, absent an agreement to the contrary. The partnership must prepare an annual information return for the IRS known as *Schedule K-1, Form 1065*, which the IRS uses to check against the individual returns filed by the partners. This form details each partner's share of income, credits, and deductions.

LIMITED PARTNERSHIPS

The *limited partnership* (LP)—not to be confused with the *limited liability partnership* described later—is a hybrid containing elements of both partnerships and corporations. A limited partnership may be formed by parties who wish to invest in a business and share in its profits, but seek to limit their risk to the amount of their investment. The law provides such limited risk for the limited partner, but only so long as the limited partner plays no active role in the day-to-day management and operation of the business. In effect, the limited partner is very much like an investor who buys a few shares of stock in a corporation, but has no significant role in running the business.

Health care professionals are most likely to employ a limited partnership structure when one of the professionals retires or becomes incapacitated and the partners agree to allow that partner to remain as an inactive member of the partnership until a full separation is completed. Before entering into a limited partnership with a nonprofessional or a professional who practices a different profession than that of the practice, you should contact your professional licensing authority to determine whether it is permissible for your practice to have such owners.

Formation

In order to establish a limited partnership, it is necessary to have one or more *general partners* who run the practice (and have full personal liability) and one or more *limited partners* who play a passive role. Forming a limited partnership requires documentation to be filed with the proper state agency. If the documents are not filed or are improperly filed, a limited partner could be treated as a general partner and lose the benefit of limited liability. In addition, the limited partner must refrain from becoming involved in the day-to-day operation of the partnership. Otherwise, the limited partner might be found to be actively participating in the business and could be held to be a general partner with unlimited personal liability.

Uses

A limited partnership is a convenient business form for securing needed financial backers who wish to share in the profits of an enterprise without undue exposure to personal liability.

IN PLAIN ENGLISH

A limited partnership can be used to attract investors when credit is hard to get or is too expensive. In return for investing, the limited partner may receive a designated share of the profits. From the entrepreneur's point of view, this may be an attractive way to fund a business, since the limited partner receives nothing if there are no profits. Had the entrepreneur borrowed money from a creditor, he or she would be at risk to repay the loan regardless of the success or failure of the business.

Another use of the limited partnership is to facilitate reorganization of a general partnership after the death or retirement of a general partner. Remember, a partnership can be terminated upon the request of any partner. Although the original partnership is technically dissolved when one partner retires, it is not uncommon for the remaining partners to agree to *buy out* the retiring partner's share—that is, to return that person's capital contribution and keep the practice going. Some state laws establish this as the rule unless the parties agree otherwise.

Raising enough cash to buy out the retiring partner, however, could jeopardize the business by forcing the remaining partners to liquidate certain partnership assets. A convenient way to avoid such a detrimental liquidation is for the retiree to step into a limited partner status. Thus, he or she can continue to share in the profits (which, to some extent, flow from that partner's past labor), while removing personal assets from the risk of partnership liabilities. In the meantime, the remaining partners are afforded the opportunity to restructure the partnership funding under more favorable terms.

WHAT YOU DO NOT WANT: UNINTENDED PARTNERS

Whether yours is a straightforward general partnership or a limited partnership, one arrangement you want to avoid is the *unintended partnership*. This can occur when you work together with another person and your relationship is not described formally. There are cases in which professionals have been held liable for the acts of other independent professionals where it appeared to third persons that they were partners even though in reality they were not. In *Hill v. St. Clare's Hospital*, a patient sought medical care from a physician who conducted an independent practice but rendered services along with other physicians under a common name. When the care rendered was deemed negligent, the patient sued. It was held that all the physicians doing business under the common name were liable as if they were partners despite the fact that they were only sharing office space. Important to the court were the facts that the physicians conducted their practices under a single, common name, and had a consolidated accounting system including billing, a single letterhead listing all the physicians who shared space in the office, a single phone number that was answered with the clinic's name, and a clinic bank account out of which each independent physician drew amounts due for work performed.

To minimize this kind of exposure, health care professionals who merely share office space should take care to avoid giving the impression that the individual practitioners are engaged in any form of group practice. They should post a sign in their waiting room making it clear that individuals in the office practice independently from one another in treating their own patients and are not members of a group practice. Patients should be provided with a similar written notice as part of their signed intake form. Each practitioner should have a different phone number from the other practitioners that should be answered by using that particular professional's name. If a single number is desired, then a more generic greeting such as, "Physicians' offices," or the like should be used. Each practitioner should have a separate bank account and render his or her billings on an individualized letterhead. Neither a common name nor a consolidated letterhead should be used. Patient charts should be separated, and each practitioner should prepare an individualized fee schedule.

CORPORATIONS

The word *corporation* may call to mind a vision of a large company with hundreds or thousands of employees. In fact, the vast majority of corporations in the United States are small or moderate-sized companies. There are, of course, advantages and disadvantages to incorporating. If it appears advantageous to incorporate, you will find it can be done with surprising ease and little expense. You should, however, use the services of a knowledgeable business lawyer to ensure compliance with state formalities and completion of corporate mechanics, and to obtain advice on corporate taxation. Note that in many states, health care professionals who desire to use a corporate structure must register as a *professional corporation* (PC) rather than as a *business* or *not-for-profit corporation*. A PC is similar to a business corporation but does not offer the same degree of protection against liability arising from professional negligence.

Corporations Compared to Partnerships

In describing the corporate form, it is useful to compare it to a partnership.

Liability

Perhaps the most important difference is that the owners of the corporation are not, as a rule, personally liable for the corporation's debts. They stand to lose only their investments. Unlike a limited partner, a *shareholder* is allowed full participation in the control of the corporation through his or her voting privileges—the higher the percentage of outstanding shares owned, the more significant the control.

For the small health care professional corporation, however, limited liability may be something of an illusion. Very often, creditors will require that the owners personally cosign for any credit extended, including credit cards. In addition, individuals remain responsible for their own wrongful acts. Thus, a shareholder who is found guilty of professional negligence (*malpractice*) will not only subject the practice to liability, but also remains personally liable. All of the shareholder's *personal assets* (for example, house and car) are at risk to satisfy the judgment against him or her.

Where one shareholder is guilty of negligence or misconduct, most state statutes limit the other shareholders' liability to their investment in the corporation. However, a minority of states hold all shareholders liable for each other's professional liability or misconduct. In other words, if one shareholder is found guilty of malpractice, all shareholders can be held personally liable to satisfy the judgment. In these few states, the other shareholders' liability remains limited with regard to other potential exposures such as debts and other contractual obligations.

The *corporate shield* also offers protection in situations where an agent hired by the corporation has committed a wrongful act while working for the corporation. For example, if your computer consultant negligently injures a pedestrian while driving to the store to purchase a new monitor for your practice, the consultant will be liable for the wrongful act and the corporation may be liable; however, the shareholder who owns stock in the corporation will probably not be held personally liable.

To retain the liability shield, certain corporate formalities must be strictly adhered to so as to establish the corporation as a separate legal entity. These include having a separate bank account for the corporation, even if it has only one shareholder, and ensuring that corporate and personal funds are not commingled.

Continuity of Existence

Another difference between a corporation and a partnership relates to continuity of existence. Since there is often a frequent turnover of members in a group practice, this is an important factor. Many of the events that can cause the dissolution of a partnership do not have the same effect on a corporation. In fact, it is common for a corporation to have perpetual existence. Shareholders, unlike partners, cannot decide to withdraw and demand a return of capital from the corporation—all they can do is sell their stock. A corporation may, therefore, have both legal and economic continuity.

IN PLAIN ENGLISH

A corporation's continuity can be a tremendous disadvantage to shareholders (or their heirs) if they want to sell stock when there are no buyers for it. *Buy-sell agreements* can, however, be made between the shareholders and the corporation to guarantee return of capital to the estate of a shareholder who dies, to a shareholder who decides to withdraw, or to a shareholder who becomes incapacitated.

Transferability of Ownership

The third difference relates to transferability of ownership. No one can become a partner without the unanimous consent of the other partners, unless otherwise agreed. In a corporation, shareholders can generally sell all or any number of their shares to whomever and whenever they wish. If the owners of a small corporation do not want it to be open to outside ownership, however, transferability may be restricted by agreement of the shareholders.

Health care professionals who have incorporated their practice must be aware of a significant limitation to the transfer of stock ownership that is common throughout most states—the purchaser of the shares must be a licensed member of the profession. There are some qualifications to this limitation that vary from state to state. In the majority of states, the shareholders need not be employees, but other states require that shareholders also be former or present employees of the corporation, or individuals who will be employees within thirty days of the issuance of shares to them. Some states allow the corporation to consist of a combination of licensed health care professionals. For example, the shareholders of the corporation may consist of doctors, nurses, dentists, and other health care professionals. Most states allow the corporation to render only one type of professional service—for example, medical care only or dental care only. A handful of state corporate statutes permit a crossover of professional services; yet, even in these states, the licensing boards may prohibit the blending of health care professionals with other professionals. For example, lawyers or accountants are customarily not permitted to own stock in medical corporations.

In states where shareholders of a health care corporation are not required to be members of the profession in which the corporation is engaged, their rights as shareholders may be limited. The state may limit their voting rights or their ability to participate in the earnings or affairs of the corporation. Nonprofessional shareholders might be allowed to be directors or officers of the corporation as long as at least 51% of the shareholders and directors of the corporation are licensed within the corporation's specialty.

Management and Control

The fourth difference is in the structure of management and control. Common shareholders are given a vote in proportion to their ownership in the corporation. Other kinds of stock can be created, with or without voting rights. A voting shareholder uses his or her vote to elect a board of directors and to create rules under which the board will operate.

The basic rules of the corporation are stated in its *articles of incorporation,* which are filed with the state. These serve as the constitution for the corporation and can be amended by shareholder vote. More detailed operational rules—*bylaws*—should also be prepared. Both shareholders and directors may have the power to create or amend bylaws. This varies from state to state and may be determined by the shareholders themselves. The *board of directors* then makes operational decisions for the corporation, typically delegating day-to-day control to a president or chief executive officer.

A shareholder, even one who owns all the stock, may not preempt a decision of the board of directors. If the board has exceeded the powers granted to it by the articles or bylaws, any shareholder may sue for a court order remedying the situation. If the board is within its powers, the shareholders then have no recourse except to remove the board or any board member. In many small businesses, the shareholders and board members are the same people, in which case this would, of course, not be a problem. In a few more progressive states, a small corporation may entirely forego having a board of directors. In these cases, the corporation is authorized to allow the shareholders to vote directly on business decisions, just as in a partnership.

Raising Additional Capital

The fifth distinction between partnerships and corporations is the greater variety of means available to the corporation for raising additional capital. Partnerships are quite restricted in this regard. They can borrow money or, if all the partners agree, they can take on additional partners. A corporation, on the other hand, may issue more stock. This stock can be of many different varieties—recallable at a set price, for example, or convertible into another kind of stock.

A process frequently used to attract a new investor is the *issuance of preferred stock*. The corporation agrees to pay the preferred shareholder some predetermined amount, known as a *dividend preference*, before it pays any dividends to other shareholders. It also means that if the corporation should go bankrupt, the preferred shareholder will generally be paid out of the proceeds of liquidation before the common shareholders, although after the corporation's creditors are paid.

In most cases, the issuance of new stock merely requires approval by a majority of the existing shareholders. In addition, corporations can borrow money on a short-term basis by issuing notes or for a longer period by issuing debentures or bonds.

IN PLAIN ENGLISH

A corporation's ability to raise additional capital is limited only by its lawyer's creativity and the economics of the marketplace.

Taxes

The last major distinction between corporations and partnerships is taxation. Under both state and federal laws, the profits of a *C corporation* are taxed to the corporation before they are paid out as dividends. Then, because the dividends constitute income to the shareholders, they are taxed again as the shareholder's personal income. This double taxation constitutes the major disadvantage of conducting business as a C corporation.

Avoiding Double Taxation

There are several methods of avoiding double taxation. First, a corporation can plan its business so as not to have much profit. This can be done by drawing off what would be profit in payments to shareholders for a variety of services. For example, a shareholder can be paid a salary, rent for property leased to the corporation, or interest on a loan made to the corporation. All of these are legal deductions from the corporate income.

Deducting Benefits

A corporation can also deduct the cost of various benefits provided for its employees. For example, a corporation can deduct all its payments made for certain qualified employee life insurance plans, while the employees pay no personal income tax on this benefit. Sole proprietors or partnerships, on the other hand, may not be entitled to deduct these expenses, or may be able to deduct only a percentage of these expenses.

Retained Earnings

A corporation can also reinvest its profits for reasonable business expansion. This undistributed money is not taxed as income to the shareholders, though the corporation must pay corporate tax on it. By contrast, the retained earnings of a partnership are taxed to the individual partners even though the money is not distributed.

Corporate reinvestment has two advantages. First, the business can be built up with money that has been taxed only at the corporate level and on which no individual shareholder needs to pay any tax. Second, within reasonable limits, the corporation can delay the distribution of corporate earnings until, for example, a time of lower personal income of the shareholder and, therefore, lower personal tax rates.

If, however, the IRS deems the amount withheld for expansion to be unreasonably high, then the corporation may be exposed to a penalty. It is, therefore, wise to work with an experienced tax planner on a regular basis.

S CORPORATIONS

Congress created a hybrid organizational form that allows the owners of a small corporation to take advantage of many of the corporate features described previously, but that is taxed in a manner similar to a sole proprietorship or partnership (thus avoiding most of the double-taxation problems). In this form of organization, called an *S corporation,* income and losses flow directly to shareholders and the corporation pays no income tax. This form can be particularly advantageous in the early years of a corporation, because the owners can deduct almost all the corporate losses from their personal incomes. They cannot do so in a C corporation. They can have this favorable tax situation while simultaneously enjoying the limited liability of the corporate form.

IN PLAIN ENGLISH

If the corporation is likely to sustain major losses and shareholders have other sources of income against which they wish to write off those losses, the S corporation is likely to be a desirable form for the business.

A *small corporation,* as defined by the tax law, does not refer to the amount of business generated; rather, it refers to the number of owners. In order to qualify for S status, the corporation may not have more than one hundred owners, each of whom must be a human being (who is either a U.S. citizen or a resident alien), an estate, or a certain kind of trust or nonprofit corporation. Additionally, there cannot be more than one class of voting stock. An S corporation can own stock in another S corporation.

Taxes

The taxation of an S corporation is similar to that of a partnership or sole proprietorship. Unfortunately, the tax rules for S corporations are not as simple as those for partnerships or individuals. Generally speaking, the owner of an S corporation can be taxed on his or her pro rata share of the distributable profits and may deduct his or her share of distributable losses.

LIMITED LIABILITY COMPANIES

The newest business form is the *limited liability company*, or LLC. This business form combines the limited liability features of a corporation with all the tax advantages available to the sole proprietor or partnership. The law in most states permits those conducting business as an LLC to create the most flexible and user-friendly organizational structure. They can elect to have the LLC's business conducted by a manager or by the *members* (owners) themselves. They may, but are not required to, have periodic meetings, and in fact, the owners can, through the *operating agreement* (equivalent to a corporation's bylaws), create whatever organizational structure they consider appropriate.

A health care professional conducting business through an LLC can shield his or her personal assets from the risk of the business for all situations except the individual's own wrongful acts. This liability shield is identical to the one offered by the corporate form. The owners of an LLC can also enjoy all the tax features accorded to sole proprietors or partners in a partnership.

LLCs do not have the same restrictions imposed on S corporations regarding the number of owners and the type of owners (e.g., human beings or specified entities). In fact, corporations, partnerships, and other business entities can own interests in LLCs. LLCs may also have more than one class of voting ownership.

Keep in mind that the LLC form is relatively new, so there is not yet any significant body of case law interpreting the meaning of the statutes that created it. It is, however, extremely flexible and, in 1997, the Internal Revenue Code was amended to permit LLCs to be taxed like C corporations if they so choose, or like sole proprietorships and partnerships.

When LLCs were first created, many professional associations declared them analogous to business corporations and prohibited their use by professionals. The limited liability partnership (LLP) was created as a permitted business form for all professionals.

LIMITED LIABILITY PARTNERSHIPS

For businesses that have been conducted in the partnership form and desire a liability shield, the *limited liability partnership* (LLP) is available. This business form parallels the LLC in most respects. It is created by converting a partnership into an LLP, and it is available for professionals who, in many states, may not conduct business through LLCs. Licensed professionals who desire some form of liability shield but are not eligible to practice as an LLC or an LP may also create professional corporations. (See the earlier discussion of corporations.)

MINORITY OWNERS

Dissolving a corporation is not only painful because of certain tax penalties, but also because it is almost always impossible without the consent of the majority of the owners. This may be true of LLCs and LLPs, as well. If you are involved in the formation of a business entity and will be a *minority owner,* you must realize that the majority owners will have ultimate and absolute control unless minority owners take certain precautions from the start. There are numerous horror stories relating to what some majority owners have done to minority owners. Avoiding these problems is no more difficult than drafting an appropriate agreement among the owners. You should always retain your own attorney to represent you during the business entity's formation, rather than waiting until it is too late.

HYBRIDS

It is important to determine which business form will be most advantageous for your business. In addition to the business forms previously discussed, many states permit the creation of *hybrid* forms of business organization, such as *limited liability limited partnerships* (LLLPs) and *business trusts*. It is important for you to consult with an experienced business lawyer in order to determine which business forms are available in your state for your profession and which would best serve your business objectives.

CHAPTER 2

Business Organization Checklist

As discussed in the previous chapter, there is a host of business forms available for health care professionals. These forms range from the simplest—sole proprietorships—to partnerships, corporations, limited liability companies, and limited liability partnerships. The structure of your business will depend upon a number of considerations. Creating any of these business forms is a rather simple process, but to do it right and enjoy all the advantages, it is highly recommended that you consult an accountant as well as a business lawyer. Of course, the services of both cost money, but you can save some money if you come properly prepared. The following are some of the points you should be prepared to discuss.

NAMING YOUR PRACTICE

Regardless of its form, every practice will have a name. Contact your attorney ahead of time with the proposed name for your practice. A quick inquiry to the corporation commissioner or secretary of state will establish whether the proposed name is available. Many corporate divisions have online services that enable you to begin the process yourself, though it is a good idea to talk to your attorney about whether it would be appropriate to also conduct a trademark search for your chosen name.

If using a name for a sole proprietorship other than your full name, you will need to register it as an assumed business name. Depending on your state, this registration may be made through the secretary of state, county clerk, or other authority.

Most partnerships simply use the surnames of the principal partners. The choice in that case is nothing more than the order of the names—which depends on various factors from prestige to the way the names sound in a particular order. If the business name does not include the partners' full names (for example, "Smith, Jones & Henderson"), it will be necessary to file the proposed business name with the appropriate agency. Care should be taken to choose a name that is distinctive and not already in use. If the name is not distinctive, others can use it. If the name is already in use, you could be liable for trade name or trademark infringement.

In most states, if you are setting up your practice as a corporation, LLC, LP, or LLP, you or your attorney can reserve your chosen business name until you are ready to use it. You will also have to consider whether your practice will have a special mark or logo that needs trademark protection.

BUSINESS STRUCTURE

It is also important to determine which business form your practice will adopt, since each available structure has benefits and drawbacks. The business forms to consider and their pros and cons are discussed as follows and in Chapter 1.

Sole Proprietorship

The sole proprietorship is the simplest form of business. You will need to obtain any necessary business license and register any assumed business name. Although it is not required, it is a good idea for a sole proprietorship to set up a separate business bank account, especially if an assumed business name is used.

Partnership

If it is determined that you will conduct your practice in the partnership form, it is essential that you have a formal written agreement prepared by a skilled business attorney. The more time you and your prospective partners spend on being well prepared by discussing these details in advance of meeting with a lawyer, the less such a meeting is likely to cost you.

Following are the eight basic items of a partnership agreement that you should consider.

1. **Name.** Decide on the name you will use (see the previous section, "Naming Your Practice"), and identify it in the partnership agreement.

2. **Description of the Business.** In describing the business, the partners should agree on the basic scope of the practice—its requirements in regard to capital and labor, each party's individual contributions of capital and labor, and perhaps some plans regarding future growth.

3. **Capital.** After determining how much capital each partner will contribute, the partners must decide when it will be contributed, how to value the property contributed, and whether a partner can contribute or withdraw property at a later date.

4. **Duration.** Sometimes partnerships are organized for a fixed amount of time or are automatically dissolved on certain conditions, such as the completion of a project.

5. **Distribution of Profits.** You can make whatever arrangement you and your partners want for the distribution of profits. Although ordinarily a partner is not paid, it is possible to give an active partner a salary in addition to a share of the profits. Since the partnership's profits can be determined only at the close of a business year, distributions ordinarily are not made until that time. It is, however, possible to allow the partners a monthly draw of money against their share of the final profits. In some cases, it may also be necessary or desirable to allow limited expense accounts for some partners.

Not all the profits of the partnership need to be distributed at year's end. Some can be retained for expansion. This arrangement can be provided for in the partnership agreement. Whether or not the profits are distributed, all partners must pay tax on their shares of the profit. The tax code refers directly to the partnership agreement to determine what that share is, further demonstrating the importance of a partnership agreement.

6. **Management.** The power in the partnership can be divided many ways. All partners can be given the same voice or some may be given more than others. A few partners might be allowed to manage the business entirely, with the remaining partners being given a vote only on specifically designated issues.

Besides voting, three other areas of management should be covered. First is the question of who can sign checks, place orders, or enter into contracts on behalf of the partnership. Under state partnership laws, any partner may do these things as long as they occur in the usual course of business. Since such a broad delegation of authority can lead to confusion, it might be best to delegate this authority more narrowly. For instance, it is common for partners to agree that checks, orders, or contracts for more than a predetermined amount must be signed by two or more partners. Second, it is a good idea to determine a regular date for partnership meetings. Finally, some consideration should be given to the possibility of a disagreement arising among the partners that leads to a deadlock. One way to avoid this is to distribute the voting power so as to make a deadlock impossible. In a two-person partnership, however, this would mean that one partner would be in absolute control. That might be unacceptable to the other partner. If power is divided equally among an even number of partners, as is often the case, the agreement should stipulate a neutral party or arbitrator who could settle any dispute to avoid a dissolution of the partnership.

7. **Prohibited Acts.** By law, each partner owes the partnership certain duties by virtue of being an agent of the partnership. First is the *duty of diligence.* This means the partner must exercise reasonable care in acting as a partner. Second is a *duty of obedience.* The partner must obey the rules of the partnership and, most importantly, must not exceed the authority that the partnership has entrusted in him or her. Finally, there is a *duty of loyalty.* A partner may not, without approval of the other partners, compete with the partnership in business. A partner also may not seize upon a business opportunity that would be of value to the partnership without first telling the partnership about it and allowing the partnership to pursue it, if the partnership so desires. A list of prohibited acts should be made a part of the partnership agreement, elaborating and expanding on these fundamental duties.

8. **Dissolution and Liquidation.** A partnership is automatically dissolved upon the death, withdrawal, or expulsion of a partner. *Dissolution* identifies the legal end of the partnership, but need not affect its economic life if the partnership agreement has provided for the continuation of the business after a dissolution. Nonetheless, a dissolution will affect the practice, because the partner who withdraws or is expelled, or the estate of a deceased partner, will be entitled to a return of the proportionate share of capital that the departing partner contributed.

Details, such as how this capital will be returned, should be decided before dissolution. At the time of dissolution, it may be impossible to negotiate. One method of handling this is to provide for a return of the capital in cash over a period of time. Some provision should be made so that each of the remaining partners will know how much of a departing partner's interest they may purchase.

After a partner leaves, the partnership may need to be reorganized and recapitalized. Again, provisions for this should be worked out in advance if possible. Finally, since it is always possible that the partners will eventually want to liquidate the partnership, it should be decided in advance who will liquidate the assets, which assets will be distributed, and what property, if any, will be returned to its original contributor.

Corporations, LLCs, and LLPs

There are usually two reasons for creating a business form such as a corporation, LLC, or LLP—limiting personal liability and minimizing income tax liability. The second reason is generally applicable to a business that is earning a good deal of money.

IN PLAIN ENGLISH

Even if your business is not earning much money, you may nevertheless want to consider creating a business entity that limits your personal liability.

Corporations, LLCs, and LLPs are hypothetical legal persons, and as such, are responsible for their own acts and contracts. Thus, if a patient trips in your waiting room or if your receptionist negligently injures a pedestrian while driving to pick up supplies for your corporation, LLC, or LLP, your practice—not its owners—will be liable, assuming the proper formalities have been adhered to.

NOTE: Any individual personally responsible for a wrongful act will also be liable.

OFFICERS AND OWNERS

State statutes generally require a corporation, LLC, or LLP to have a *chief operating officer*, such as a president or manager. In addition, state statutes may require other administrative officers, such as a secretary. The corporate bylaws or the LLC's or LLP's operating agreement should have a separate description for specialized officers. Note that most states permit LLCs to elect to be run by a single manager or by the *members* (owners).

Owners

Questions to ask yourself regarding owners include the following.

- How many shares of stock should your corporation be authorized to issue? (In the case of LLCs and LLPs, *certificates of ownership*, which resemble shares of stock in a corporation, are used.)

- For a corporation, how many units should be issued when the practice commences operations?

- For a corporation, how many units of stock should be held in reserve for future issuance?

- Should there be separate classes of owners?

If the corporation or LLC is to be family-owned, ownership may be used to some extent as a means of estate planning or wealth-shifting. You might, therefore, also wish to ask your attorney about updating your will at the same time you incorporate or create an LLC. While LLPs may be used for this purpose, it is not as common.

Owner Agreements

Discuss with your lawyer the possibility of creating owner agreements that govern the employment status of key individuals or commit owners to voting a certain way on specific issues. Ensure that a method has been established to prevent an owners' voting deadlock.

Buy-Sell Agreements

The first meeting with your lawyer is a good time to discuss buy-sell agreements. *Buy-sell agreements* resolve such matters as what happens when one of the owners wishes to leave the practice or under what circumstances an owner is able to sell to outsiders. In closely held corporations, the corporation or other shareholders are generally granted the first option to buy the stock. The same kind of procedure can be implemented for LLCs and LLPs.

Decide what circumstances should trigger the practice's or other owners' right to buy the interest—death, disability, retirement, termination, and so forth. Also decide whether the buy-sell agreement should be tied to insurance on the lives of key persons that would fund the purchase of their ownership interests by the corporation, LLC, or LLP in the event of their deaths. A buy-sell agreement can also identify the mechanism for valuing the practice—annual appraisal, book value, multiple earnings, arbitration, or some other method—when an owner departs.

Planning for Future Owners

If you anticipate bringing in some additional owners, you and your attorney should discuss the method by which this may be accomplished. There are legal restrictions that are imposed on the issuance and sale of additional shares of stock and the sale and transfer of LLC or LLP interests. Planning for the future is best done at formation.

Governing Board

An initial decision must be made as to who will be on the board of directors of a corporation or the governing board of an LLC or LLP and how many initial directors there will be. You must also decide whether owners will have the right to elect members of the board based on their percentages of ownership. If the LLC or LLP elects to be run by a manager, then a method for selecting that person should be specified.

IN PLAIN ENGLISH

It is a good idea to have an odd number of directors or managers in order to avoid the potential for a voting deadlock.

CAPITALIZATION

At this point, the attorney works closely with your accountant. Issues to resolve include the following, all of which may have tax consequences.

- What will be the initial capitalization or funding of the corporation, LLC, or LLP?

- What is being contributed by owners in exchange for their interests— money, past services, equipment, assets of an ongoing business, licensing agreements, or other things?

- Will owners make loans to the business?

- What value will be placed on assets that are contributed to the practice?

HOUSEKEEPING

Your attorney and accountant will need to know several other details. For instance, the number of employees the business anticipates for the coming twelve-month period must be stated on the application for a federal taxpayer identification number. You must also decide whether the business tax year will end on December 31 or on another date.

> **NOTE:** S corporations and LLCs that are not taxable entities must adopt the calendar year.

A decision on whether the practice's accounting method will be on a cash basis or accrual basis must be made. The amount of salaries for its officers or managers, if any, must be authorized. The date for the annual meeting must be set. Selecting a *registered agent* (generally, your attorney will assume this role) and determining which bank your practice will use are all preliminary decisions that must be made.

EMPLOYEE BENEFITS

Be prepared to consider *employee benefit plans*, such as life and health insurance, profit-sharing, a pension, or other retirement plans, and employee ownership programs, as well as other fringe benefits. Even if you do not plan to implement such programs when the corporation, LLC, or LLP is created, it is nonetheless a good idea to consider whether such programs may be instituted in the future.

TAX TREATMENT

Like corporations, LLCs and LLPs can elect to be taxed like C corporations, or choose to be mere conduits, passing income and expense directly to the owners. There are requirements for when such an election must be filed. Be sure to discuss this issue with your accountant either before or immediately after creating your LLC or LLP. The same is true for filing an S election. Careful consideration must be given to the appropriate tax treatment, as you may not be able to change your decision later.

If your practice is likely to sustain major losses and owners have other sources of income against which they wish to write off those losses, chances are a pass-through entity would be appropriate.

As you can see, there is much to discuss at the first meeting with your lawyer. A little time and thought prior to that meeting will prove to be a worthwhile investment.

CHAPTER 3

Advertising

Advertising by health care professionals is a phenomenon that only began in the late 1970s. Prior to this time, both legal and ethical barriers inhibited practitioners from developing advertising programs for their practices. Early on, professional associations themselves placed strict limitations on all forms of advertising and solicitation. Traditionally, this self-regulation was carried out through the promulgation of an ethical code that strongly discouraged practitioners from advertising and soliciting patients. In addition, these admonitions were frequently reflected in state licensure laws. These self-imposed restrictions were the result of concern over an increased likelihood of deception, which stemmed from the high degree of consumer dependence on health care professionals. In addition to this paternalistic motivation, most practitioners themselves simply viewed advertising as unprofessional and demeaning to the health care professions.

Today, fewer practitioners and professional associations still view advertising with skepticism and apprehension. Additionally, several court decisions have significantly curtailed the ability of professional associations to prohibit their respective members from advertising.

IN PLAIN ENGLISH

Old Rule: Advertising was unseemly, demeaning, and unprofessional. It was bound to degrade the services of a learned profession by forcing doctors to hawk their services like any other item of trade. Patients would be bombarded with commercial solicitations to try out different doctors and different services until no physician would be able to maintain a proper and productive long-term physician-patient relationship.

Current Rule: Advertise if you want to, but don't tell lies or make statements that might deceive patients.

Prior to 1975, the *American Medical Association* (AMA) essentially forbade any form of advertising or solicitation by its members. In that year, the *Federal Trade Commission* (FTC) challenged an AMA affiliate's advertising restrictions. While litigation was pending, the AMA issued a statement that evidenced a significant change in policy. Essentially, the statement declared that, while solicitation was still strictly forbidden, advertising was allowed under certain circumstances.

The FTC refused to drop its complaint, even though the AMA had signaled an intent to change its policy. In the case *In the Matter of the American Medical Association* (Docket No. 9064 (1982)), the FTC contended that the AMA affiliate's regulations restrained competition. The administrative law judge agreed with the FTC's position and ordered the AMA to cease and desist its illegal activities; however, the opinion was quite vague with respect to the restrictions that still were permissible.

In 1980, a federal court affirmed the FTC's ruling and clarified which restrictions were still permissible in *American Medical Association v. Federal Trade Commission*, 638 F.2d 443 (2d Cir. 1980). The court stated that the AMA could still "adopt guidelines . . . with respect to representations that the AMA reasonably believes to be false or deceptive." In other words, the AMA cannot prohibit advertising completely, but it can regulate advertising that is false or deceptive. In 1982, the United States Supreme Court considered this issue; however, the Court was split four to four. Accordingly, the lower court ruling was affirmed but no opinion was written. With no opinion from the Supreme Court, we are left with the rule from the lower court that professional association and licensing boards can regulate false or deceptive advertising but not impose a complete ban on advertising.

GOVERNMENT REGULATION

Representations about a product or service must be truthful and not likely to deceive the consumer. States have consumer protection laws and the FTC and *Food and Drug Administration* (FDA) each issue regulations on advertising to protect consumers. Although professional associations may also restrict such advertising, the associations are limited to expulsion of the member from the association as a penalty for engaging in false or deceptive advertising.

IN PLAIN ENGLISH

You should be aware that the rules regarding the advertising of health care services vary from state to state, although false or misleading advertisements are universally prohibited. Beyond that rule, states may impose different and more particular requirements. One state may accept the term "board certified" in a very general way, while another will require a doctor to have passed a specific kind of board examination from a specific kind of board in order to use that description of qualification in his or her ads. You should, therefore, consult with an attorney in your state about the content of your advertising before running it.

Note, too, that health care professionals advertising on the Internet or in publications that are targeted to persons in more than one state must indicate on the advertisement the states in which the practitioner is licensed and make clear that the health care practitioner's services are available only in those states.

In addition, licensure laws in some states regulate practitioner advertising. Violation of such a law may result in the revocation of the practitioner's license to practice in that particular state. Since the regulations vary from state to state, be sure to check your particular state's restrictions.

As noted earlier, the FTC is involved in policing advertising, too; however, since the FTC is a federal agency, its jurisdiction is limited to businesses that are engaged in interstate commerce. That is to say, if your practice extends beyond your state boundaries and either touches or affects another state, then the FTC has jurisdiction over your practice.

Finally, there are special regulations pertaining to the development of a new product or service that may provide some medicinal benefits, such as a new type of therapy or a dietary supplement. Before you can advertise such a medicine or therapy, it must first be approved by the Food and Drug Administration, and advertisements for dietary supplements must follow the *Dietary Supplement Health and Education Act* (see **www.fda.gov/opacom/laws/dshea.html**) and the FTC statement "Dietary Supplements: An Advertising Guide for Industry" (see **www.ftc.gov/bcp/conline/pubs/buspubs/dietsupp.htm**). The approval process for new drugs is quite technical and will require you to work closely with a lawyer specializing in this area of practice. Failure to comply with the requirements of the FDA could subject you to fines and, in some instances, imprisonment.

IN PLAIN ENGLISH

If you develop a drug or therapy that is subject to FDA approval, the advertising of that product or service is subject to much stronger rules about how you can describe the effects of the drug or the nature of the therapy.

- Advertisements must contain warnings and descriptions of side effects.

- The phrases "Available only by prescription" and "Use only as directed by your physician" generally must appear visually within the commercial.

- Use of the product may not be depicted on-camera.

- Absent sufficient qualification or documentation, terms such as "safe," "without risk," "harmless," or words of similar meaning may not be used.

- Advertising appeals for medicines may not be made to children.

- The results of clinical trials might have to be described in a particular manner so as not to deceive the audience.

- For nonprescription drugs and over-the-counter medical devices, there is a prohibition against claims that the product alone will effect a cure.

Health care professionals should seek out the advice of a lawyer specializing in the area of FDA and FTC regulations on advertising before attempting to promote any new drug or therapy.

PROBLEM AREAS

False or misleading advertising is prohibited. Whether or not an advertisement is false is rather easy to evaluate—either the claim made can be substantiated or it cannot. Whether an advertisement is misleading or deceptive is more difficult to determine. The standard used is generally that of the *reasonable patient*. That is, would a reasonable patient be deceived by the particular claim?

Some forms of advertising are more likely to be deemed deceptive as a result of the subjective nature of the quality of services and great degree of variation in the quality of services from one practitioner to another. The following forms of advertising are those that tend to create a greater likelihood of deception and, therefore, should be used with care.

Endorsements and Testimonials

Patient endorsements and testimonials are generally closely scrutinized. Since the quality of service received by one individual may vary greatly from the quality of service another receives, there is concern over the potential for deception. A testimonial that advocates a practitioner's services and expressly or implicitly communicates benefits that are not representative of the benefits an average patient would receive could raise unwarranted expectations about the practitioner's services. Such an advertisement would very likely be considered misleading or deceptive.

Several sources, including the FTC and several professional associations, have promulgated guidelines for the use of endorsements and testimonials (e.g., **www.ftc.gov/bcp/guides/endorse.htm**). These guidelines include the following.

- The speaker's experience should reflect that of the average patient. If the experience recounted in the testimonial is not representative of the majority of patients, or if there is a great degree of variance in the benefits that may be received, this should be made clear in the advertisement.

- The testimonial should reflect the honest opinion and experience of the patient and should be made by an actual patient.

- Although the testimonial need not be phrased in the exact words of the patient, statements should not be taken out of context to imply a meaning that is different from the opinion of the patient.

- Testimonial speakers should not make objective claims concerning the safety, efficacy, benefits, or risks of a practitioner's services that cannot be soundly substantiated.

- If an expert is used to endorse the practitioner's services, the expert's opinion should be based on an actual, independent evaluation of the practitioner's services that is at least as extensive as someone with the same degree of expertise would normally conduct.

Note that this list is not exhaustive and merely presents some minimum standards.

An issue related to the use of endorsements and testimonials is the use of photographs or models to portray the benefits that may be received through use of the practitioner's services. Where models are used in such a way as to suggest that the model received the practitioner's services, the ad should clearly state that the model is only a model and did not receive the advertised services.

Before-and-after photographs are particularly susceptible to allegations of deceptive advertising—both of these photographs should use the same lighting, poses, and techniques so that the after photo is not an unrealistic portrayal of the services rendered and benefits received. Advertising text accompanying the photographs should not misrepresent the actual healing time after the procedure. In addition, when a photograph represents results that are not representative of the results an average patient would receive, the advertisement should clearly disclose this fact.

Because of intellectual property and privacy rights, you should obtain an appropriate release before using photographs or testimonials. Consult your attorney for a suitable form.

Comparative Advertising

It is quite common for businesses of all kinds to boost the merits of their products and services by comparing them to those of their competitors. This form of advertising is permissible, provided that the statements made are true. Advertisements that compare the quality of services among practitioners are dangerous, however. The quality of service given by varying practitioners is highly subjective and does not lend itself well to objective comparison. Consequently, there is a significant danger that such an advertisement may be construed as misleading. The FTC's guidelines on comparative advertising are found at **www.ftc.gov/bcp/policystmt/ad-compare.htm**.

Instead of comparing services, some practitioners simply compare fees and costs. Yet, if the fees are tied to services that vary greatly in quality, the problem of subjectivity (and the consequent propensity to mislead) arises once again. If you want to communicate your fee structure, the safer choice is to merely state your fees without making comparisons to other practitioners. Any claims you make regarding your fee structure should also indicate whether there are any collateral costs that are commonly associated with the advertised services.

Occasionally an advertiser makes disparaging remarks about the services of another. In this situation, the one who intentionally or (more commonly) negligently makes untrue, disparaging remarks about the services of another practitioner may be held legally accountable to the injured party. It should be noted that for a disparaging remark to be actionable, it must be both untrue and believable by a reasonable person. If the statement made was so outlandish as to be unbelievable, it is likely that the practitioner who was disparaged will not be able to prove any injury.

Advertising an Area of Specialization
So long as you actually have the training, experience, and competence to practice the specialty advertised, statements that hold you out as a specialist in the field are highly unlikely to be construed as misleading. Your local state board of the healing arts might have more specific recommendations or regulations on this topic, so it would be a good idea for you or your attorney to consult it.

OTHER ISSUES

Publicity Rights and Privacy Rights
Endorsements by local or national celebrities are frequently used in advertising; thus the appropriate rules deserve mention. If a celebrity endorsement is used, it is necessary to first acquire the celebrity's consent. If you do not, you may be liable to the celebrity for violating his or her *right of publicity*. This right is

granted to those who commercially exploit their names, voices, or images. In addition, the use of a look-alike or even a sound-alike stand-in for the true celebrity if used for commercial purposes (such as advertising your services) most likely will be actionable. A disclaimer or corrective explanation for the confusingly similar looks or sounds of the endorser might ameliorate the damage, but it is not a guaranteed cure for a fake endorsement.

A person who has not achieved celebrity status might be used to endorse a practitioner's services, but even if the person is not well-known, each person still possesses a *right of privacy* against the unapproved appropriation of his or her name, likeness, or persona for commercial purposes. If an individual's photograph, likeness, and so forth is not the focal point of the ad, but is merely an incidental part—such as a head in a crowd or a member of an audience—such individual's permission may not be essential before the photograph may be used in the ad. Even though you may not be required to obtain permission from the individual before using his or her photograph, it is a good idea to obtain a signed photo release whenever possible. The release should be worded in such a way as to give your business permission to use the name, likeness, or voice for any and all purposes, including advertising your practice.

Trademark

Advertisers that possess trademarks and service marks certainly will want to prominently display them in all their advertising. An advertiser may also be permitted to display the trademark of another business in an ad so long as there is no likelihood that the average reader would believe the ad was sponsored by the company whose trademark is being used. In other words, it should be a very minor, incidental use of the mark that presents no reasonable likelihood of confusion between your services and the trademark belonging to another. In these limited circumstances, you may use the other entity's trademark. Thus, it may be permissible for you to have an ad for your services that contains a photo of an individual holding a distinctively shaped Coca-Cola bottle (which is a federally registered trademark), as long as it is clear from the advertisement that the Coca-Cola Company is not the source, sponsor, or endorser of your services and as long as you do not disparage Coca-Cola.

Trademarks are everywhere, and if you are shooting an ad in a public place, a number of famous marks might reveal themselves in the photograph or footage on passing cars, billboards, storefronts, and other places. If any mark achieves a prominent place in the ad because of these fortuitous circumstances, it would not be a bad idea to digitally remove the mark from the image or footage before using the advertisement, unless you are prepared to obtain permission for the use of the mark from the mark's owner.

Copyright

Advertisements, flyers, booklets, and any textual material written or commissioned by you may be entitled to copyright protection. In fact, any original work of authorship that is put in some tangible form will likely enjoy the benefits of the federal copyright law. While copyright protection automatically attaches upon completion of a work, it is a good idea to use a copyright notice—© symbol (or the word "Copyright"); the year in which the work was first distributed to the public; and, your name. For example, "© 2008 Leonard D. DuBoff." In addition, if you register the work with the Copyright Office, you will be entitled to significant remedies if someone copies your protected material without your permission. Registration is quite simple and merely requires you to deposit two copies of the work, complete the appropriate registration form (*Form TX* in the case of textual material), and pay a forty-five dollar fee. An intellectual property attorney can assist you in identifying your copyrightable material and registering it.

Use of other persons' works, whether textual or visual, in your advertising is the other side of the copyright coin. In general, commercial uses, such as the advertising of your business, require permission for any meaningful use of words or images, even if you use only a small number of words or part of an image. If you are contemplating using anyone else's words or images in your advertising, you should consult with an intellectual property attorney who deals with copyright issues to make sure you are not infringing anyone's copyrights.

Geographic Locations and Public Places

Geographic locations may be used in advertisements without obtaining the owner's consent. Standing in front of a work of art on display indoors or outdoors, however, is not permitted unless you obtain permission of the copyright owner you determine that the copyright on the work has expired and the work is in the public domain. Buildings are now protected by copyright, though there is an exception in the law for photographs and other pictorial representations of the building so long as it is ordinarily usable from a public place. In addition, there has been at least one case holding that a very identifiable building can enjoy *trade dress protection*.

IN PLAIN ENGLISH

Posing in front of a well-known hospital or treatment center for your advertising images creates the possibility of confusion. If your practice is not affiliated with such a facility, you should avoid making a deceptive suggestion of association. Even if you use a disclaimer in your ad, the overall effect of the suggested association may be found to be deceptive.

Advertising within the health care industry remains less prevalent than in other areas of professional services. If you should choose to advertise, it is essential that your advertisements be truthful and not misrepresent the costs, efficacy, or benefits of your services. In addition, you must be careful not to violate the rights of other businesses or individuals and to protect your own. Care should be taken to work with an attorney skilled in advertising law in order to be assured of having an effective program that will enable you to promote your services without exposing yourself to liability. Having a poorly drafted advertising program will likely be more harmful than having none at all.

CHAPTER 4

People Who Work for You

There comes a time in the life of almost every health care practice when it is necessary to get help, be it brain or brawn. The help most commonly needed first is the bookkeeper/receptionist, who can handle patients, phones, billing, and the like. When things get a little hectic around the office, you might then hire someone to help with patient treatment, such as a nurse, medical assistant, or massage therapist. As your practice grows, you may soon have to hire more employees, such as, for example, a full-time lab technician or nutritionist, to keep up with increased demands.

INDEPENDENT CONTRACTORS

Someone hired on a one-time or job-by-job basis is called an *independent contractor*. Although paid for their services by the hiring firm or individual, contractors remain their own bosses and may even employ others to actually do the work.

If once or twice a year you hire an accountant to prepare your financial statements and tax returns, that person is an independent contractor. An electrician or plumber called in from time to time to work on various systems in your office is a classic example of an independent contractor. The fact that the person is independent, and not your employee, means that you do not have to pay Social Security, withhold income taxes, obtain a workers' compensation policy, or comply with the myriad rules imposed on employers. More importantly, you are generally not liable for injuries to a third party resulting from the independent contractor's negligence or wrongful acts, even while he or she is working for you. There are, however, situations where, despite your innocence, you can be rendered legally responsible for an independent contractor's wrongful acts. Such situations fall into the following three basic categories.

1. If an employer is careless in hiring an independent contractor and an appropriate investigation would have disclosed facts to indicate that the contractor was not qualified, the employer may be liable when the independent contractor fails to properly perform the job.

2. If a job is so dangerous as to be characterized as *ultrahazardous* (a legal term) and is to be performed for the employer's benefit, then, regardless of who performs the work, the employer will remain legally responsible for any injuries that occur during the performance of the work. For example, a health care professional cannot escape liability by using an X-ray technician who is an independent contractor.

3. An employer may be required by law to perform certain tasks for the health and safety of the community.

These responsibilities are said to be *nondelegable*—that is, an employer cannot delegate them and thus escape liability for their improper performance. If, therefore, a nondelegable duty is performed by an independent contractor, the employer will remain responsible for any injury that results. A good example of a nondelegable duty is the law (common in many states) that property owners are responsible for keeping their sidewalks free of dangerous obstacles. If a physician hires an independent contractor to fulfill this obligation by removing ice during the winter, the physician is still legally liable if someone is injured on the slippery sidewalk, even if the accident resulted from the contractor's carelessness.

IN PLAIN ENGLISH

There are multiple factors used in the law to determine who among the people performing services for you at your behest are independent contractors and who are employees. These factors are weighed together in a case-by-case determination; some are given heavier weight than others, and a telling score on one factor can outweigh weaker scores on other factors. The test varies slightly from state to state.

Factors That Distinguish Independent Contractors From Employees

Factor	Independent Contractors	Employees
Employment taxes, Social Security (FICA)	Employers never withhold these on behalf of true independent contractors.	If the employer is withholding these on a person's behalf, this is a huge factor favoring a finding that the person is an employee.
Place of work	More often than not, independent contractors can carry out some of their tasks away from the employer's business.	Employees tend to show up for work at the employer's place of business unless they are officially telecommuting, though some tasks might be performed at home or elsewhere from time to time.
Brings own tools	Independent contractors tend to show up with all the tools and equipment they need to do their job.	Employees more often rely on the employer to supply their tools and equipment.
Accepts direction and control over work	Independent contractors tend to have more discretion over how their work is to be performed; the employer can set the objectives, but the independent contractor usually makes the call on how to achieve the objectives.	Employees routinely accept any level of direction or control regarding how they are to perform their tasks.
Accepts new assignments	New assignments must be separately negotiated and accepted by independent contractors.	Employees routinely accept new assignments without separate discussion or negotiation.

(cont.)

| Payment | This factor is less telling, but independent contractors often are paid an hourly fee or lump sum; rarely would you call the compensation for an independent contractor a "salary." | This factor is less telling because employees might receive compensation in any number of ways—salary, hourly fee, commission, lump sum, or in other ways. |
| Continuity of employment | More often than not, independent contractors are hired for a single job or a fixed period of time. | More often than not, employees are hired to do a certain kind of job for an indefinite period of time. |

EMPLOYEES

The second capacity in which someone can work for you is as an *employee*. This category generally includes anyone over whose work you exercise direct control who is a full-time or regular part-time member of your staff. The formation of this relationship entails nothing more than an agreement on your side to hire someone and an agreement by that person to work. Although a written contract is necessary only where the contract provides for employment for more than one year, we suggest that employment terms be put down in writing so that there is no misunderstanding later. Often a simple letter will suffice for this purpose.

You will be *vicariously liable* for the negligence and sometimes even the intentional wrongdoing of your employee when the employee is acting on your behalf. This means that if your employee is on the job and is involved in an automobile accident that is his or her fault, you, as well as your employee, could be legally liable. It would be wise to be extremely careful when hiring and to contact your insurance agent to obtain sufficient insurance coverage for your additional exposure.

This chapter is, of course, important to employers, but even if you work for a health maintenance organization (HMO) or otherwise perform your job as an employee, the discussion that follows is relevant to you so that you know what rights you have as an employee.

EMPLOYMENT CONTRACTS

While there is no prescribed form that the contract must take, there are nevertheless certain items that should be considered.

Term

The first item of an employment contract is the term of employment. An employment contract may be either terminable at will or for a fixed duration. If the employment is to be for more than one year, there must be a written contract specifying the period of employment. If there is no agreed-upon term, either party may terminate the relationship at any time, and no written agreement is necessary.

Making the contract for a fixed period gives the employee some job security and creates a moral and contractual obligation for the employee to remain for the term. Of course, if the employee chooses to quit, or the employer chooses to fire the employee, the law will not compel fulfillment of the contract. Enforced servitude was outlawed along with all other forms of slavery in the nineteenth century. Improper termination of a contract for a fixed period, however, will subject the party who is responsible for the wrongful act to liability for damages.

Wage

The second item is the wage. If your practice has annual gross revenues of $500,000 or more, or if you are engaged in interstate commerce such as selling goods or services across state lines, you will have to comply with federal minimum-wage laws, but even if federal law does not apply, most states have their own minimum-wage laws with which you still will have to comply. Minimum wages imposed by the states are often significantly higher than those required by the federal government. Above the requirement imposed by this law, the amount of remuneration is open to bargaining.

In the event no salary is specified, the law will presume a reasonable wage for the work performed. Thus you cannot escape paying your employees fairly by not discussing the amount they will earn. If you hire a nurse and the accepted salary in your region for a qualified nurse is $45 per hour, it will be presumed that the nurse was hired for this amount unless you and that person have agreed to a different salary.

Note that state and federal laws require overtime compensation when a nonexempt employee works more than a certain number of hours in a day or week (depending on the state). There are significant penalties for failure to fully comply with overtime laws. You should contact your local department of labor or your attorney for information about the rules in your area.

In addition to an hourly wage or monthly salary, other benefits can be given, such as health and life insurance and retirement plans. The cost of professional liability insurance may also be paid by the employer. If this is the case, the employment contract should specify which party will purchase post-employment, or *tail*, coverage at the termination of employment. If it is not specified, then there is case law holding that the employer is required to purchase insurance. Some legal advice may be necessary in connection with benefit plans in order to take advantage of tax laws.

Duties

Third, it is often wise to spell out your employee's duties in the employment contract. This serves as a form of orientation for the employee and also may limit future conflicts over what is and what is not involved in the job. It is always a good idea to include a statement that the employee will perform other duties as directed by his or her supervisor.

Noncompetition

Fourth, you may want your employee to agree not to work for someone else while working for you or, more importantly, not to compete against you at the end of the employment period. The latter agreement must be carefully drawn to be enforceable. Such an agreement:

- must not be overly broad with respect to the kind of work the employee may not do;

- must cover a geographic area no broader than that in which you actually operate; and,

- must be for a reasonable duration (often two or three years).

Thus, if you hire a young associate to assist you with your practice, it is a good idea to contact your attorney to talk about a *noncompetition agreement* prior to the commencement of the relationship.

State laws often limit or impose conditions on noncompetition agreements. Some states, such as California, prohibit noncompetition agreements except in instances of the sale of a business. Some states require that the agreement be entered into before commencing employment or not until after a job promotion. Others have specific provisions addressing the permissible scope and duration of the agreements. Oregon, for instance, now permits noncompetition agreements only for exempt employees earning more than a certain amount per year, though there is an exception if an employer separately pays the employee a statutorily required amount for the noncompetition agreement. Further, the employer must have a *protectable interest* as defined by the statute, and the noncompetition period cannot exceed two years.

In addition, some professional associations frown on the use of restrictive covenants. You should, therefore, contact your local professional association to determine its position on this situation and whether there are guidelines or recommendations promulgated by the association.

Confidentiality Agreements and Intellectual Property

Noncompetition agreements, where they are permitted, can prevent direct forms of competition within a certain geographical region and for a limited time, but your practice may involve intellectual property such as trade secrets that you would not want any employee to use outside the scope of his or her employment while it lasts, at any time now or in the future, or in any location. A *confidentiality agreement* may be used to prohibit the use of any of your trade secrets both during the employment and after it has ended. Such an agreement should be in writing. Trade secrets may include, among other things, patient lists, supplier lists, secret formulas, secret treatment procedures, and know how. These agreements are generally permissible even in states prohibiting or limiting noncompetition agreements.

Termination

Finally, grounds for termination of the employment contract should be listed. Even if the contract is terminable at will, these grounds serve as useful benchmarks to guide your employee's actions. Unlike the situation where you have hired an independent contractor, you are *vicariously liable* for the negligence and, sometimes, even the intentional wrongdoing of your employee when the employee is acting on your behalf. That means that if your employee is on the job and is involved in an automobile accident that is his or her fault, you, as well as your employee, are legally liable. It would be wise to be extremely careful when hiring and to contact your insurance agent to obtain sufficient insurance coverage for your additional exposure.

Employers should take some precautions to avoid being placed in the untenable position of having bound themselves to individuals in their employment when the relationship has soured. This can happen even without a written employment agreement. It may result from language in employee handbooks that might be construed as giving rise to a contractual right or from oral statements made by recruiters or interviewers. To avoid this problem, an employer should have a legend placed in any employment handbook making it clear that the material is not an employment contract and should require new employees to sign a statement making it clear that the employment is at will and does not give rise to any contractual right.

If there is a probationary period, the employer should be careful to state that the employee will become a regular or full-time employee rather than a permanent employee at the end of the probation period. In addition, if there is any evaluation of the employee after the probationary period has ended, it should be conducted fairly. When evaluations become merely pro forma, problems can and do arise. For instance, employees may argue that they have received sparkling evaluations and are being fired for an unlawful reason.

OTHER CONSIDERATIONS IN HIRING

There are other issues you should consider when hiring an employee, many of which fall into the realm of accounting or bookkeeping responsibilities. You should, therefore, consult with your accountant or bookkeeper regarding items such as the following.

- A workers' compensation policy for your employees in the event of on-the-job injury or occupational illness. State laws vary on the minimum number of employees that triggers this very important requirement. Many states' workers' compensation laws provide that an employer who has failed to obtain or keep in force required workers' compensation insurance will be strictly liable, even in the absence of negligence, for on-the-job injury or illness, including not only medical expenses, but also damages for pain and suffering, lost earning potential, and other damages that are a consequence of injuries.

- Withholding taxes—federal, state, and local. Here, too, the laws vary, and you must find out what is required in your locale. Employers are required to withhold employee's federal taxes, and failure to do so will expose the employer to liability for that amount plus interest and penalties.

- Social Security (FICA).

- Unemployment insurance, both federal and state. These also include certain technical requirements for subcontractors and the like.

- Health and safety regulations, both federal and state.

- Municipal taxes for specific programs such as schools or public transportation.

- Employee benefits such as insurance coverage (medical, dental, and legal), retirement benefits, memberships, parking, and so on.

- Union requirements, if your employees are subject to union contracts.

- Wage and hour laws, both federal and state. These include minimum wage and overtime requirements. In some states, the law also regulates holidays and vacations, as well as the method and timing of paying employees during employment and upon termination.

HAZARDS IN THE WORKPLACE

While few medical professionals would intentionally injure a fellow human being, it is not uncommon for those working in a health care practice to use hazardous materials or be exposed to dangerous substances. Often employees are not aware of the potential hazard that may result from such exposure. It is advisable to research the potentially dangerous nature of all substances used in your practice, whether they are labeled for toxicity or not. You must disclose to your employees at hiring any pertinent information regarding hazardous substances. The *Occupational Safety and Health Administration* (OSHA) regulations require that all employers with hazardous chemicals in their workplace provide labels and *Material Safety Data Sheets* (MSDS) for their exposed workers and train them to handle the chemicals appropriately. (More information on this can be found at the OSHA website at **www.osha.gov/SLTC/hazardcommunications/ index.html**.)

Care with hazardous materials is particularly important today with the prevalence of the HIV virus at all levels of society. With respect to blood-borne diseases in particular, the law requires employers to establish a fairly rigorous safety program. The program must include, among other things, education and acquiring equipment, and in addition there are certain optional procedures. The employer must also keep accurate records of each employee's physical condition in order to determine whether the employee has contracted any blood-related diseases.

If an employment contract is used, a paragraph containing a disclosure of and the employee's acknowledgment of the known risks of hazardous substances in the workplace should be incorporated in the contract. A similar statement should also be included in any employment handbook. While these documents would not provide a defense to a workers' compensation claim, they would sensitize employees to the need for caution in working with hazardous substances. Needless to say, you must take all precautions possible to protect the health and safety of your employees.

Congress and federal administrative agencies are becoming more active in the regulation of hazardous substances. You should also be aware that your state workers' compensation agency or state OSHA may have passed special rules regarding specific workplace substances and activities. It is critical to obtain a lawyer's opinion as to whether any of these regulations apply to your practice. Your state's labor department may also be able to give you information regarding applicable workplace regulations.

DISCRIMINATION

There are federal and state prohibitions against discrimination in hiring, promotion, and termination. Employers must comply with numerous federal antidiscrimination laws, including the *Civil Rights Act*, the *Equal Pay Act*, the *Age Discrimination in Employment Act* (amended by the *Older Workers Benefit Protection Act*), and the *Americans With Disabilities Act*. The *Equal Employment Opportunity Commission* (EEOC) is responsible for the enforcement of these laws. The federal Civil Rights Act prohibits discrimination on the basis of race, color, religion, sex, or national origin. Antidiscrimination laws apply not only during the hiring processes, but also during the employment itself, including considerations for transfer, promotion, layoff, and termination, as well as job advertisements, recruitment, testing, use of company facilities, training, benefits, and leave. These laws generally prohibit not only intentional discrimination, but also practices that have the effect of discrimination. It is worthwhile to note that many antidiscrimination laws apply to independent contractors as well as to employees.

Many states, as well as some cities and counties, have also passed laws that reiterate and expand the federal government's protection against discrimination. These laws often are more protective of employees than the federal laws. In addition, some categories not covered by federal law, including those with respect to sexual orientation and sexual identity, may be covered by state or local law. This area is quite complex, and you should consult your attorney before establishing any employment policies and procedures.

These laws make it clear that management may not legally retaliate against employees or job applicants who file discrimination charges against them. If a business is found to have unlawfully discriminated, then that business will likely be liable for lost wages and punitive and other damages, including attorney fees.

Civil Rights Act

The federal *Civil Rights Act* is designed to address discrimination on the basis of race, color, religion, sex, or national origin. With regard to religious discrimination, employers generally may not treat employees or applicants less or more favorably because of their religious beliefs or practices. Employees cannot be forced to participate or to not participate in a religious activity as a condition of employment. Employers must reasonably accommodate employees' sincerely held religious beliefs and permit employees to engage in religious expression if employees are permitted to engage in other personal expressions at work. This law also requires the employer to take steps to prevent religious harassment of his or her employees, not only by other employees and management, but also by vendors and customers.

National origin discrimination includes discrimination based on foreign accents and English fluency, as well as English-only rules, though there are exceptions if such rules are necessary for the safe or efficient operation of the business.

Race-based discrimination includes discrimination based on skin color, hair texture, and facial features, as well as harassment and segregation. It also includes discrimination based on a person's marriage to or association with those of a different race.

The prohibitions against sex-based discrimination encompass pregnancy, birth, and related medical conditions, as well as sexual harassment (discussed later in this chapter).

Equal Pay Act

The *Equal Pay Act* (part of the *Fair Labor Standards Act of 1938*, as amended) also prohibits sex-based discrimination. It prohibits sex-based wage discrimination among persons in the same establishment who are performing under similar working conditions. Virtually all employees are subject to this act.

Age Discrimination in Employment Act

The *Age Discrimination in Employment Act* (ADEA) protects individuals who are 40 years of age or older from employment discrimination based on age. The ADEA applies to employers with at least twenty employees. The protections apply both to employees and job applicants. Under the ADEA, it is unlawful to discriminate against a person because of his or her age with respect to any aspect of employment, including hiring and firing, compensation and benefits, promotion, firing, layoffs, job assignments, and training.

The *Older Workers Benefit Protection Act of 1990* (OWBPA) amends the ADEA to include specific prohibitions against the denial of benefits to older employees.

Americans With Disabilities Act

The *Americans with Disabilities Act* (ADA) prohibits private employers from discriminating against qualified individuals with disabilities in job application procedures, hiring and firing, compensation and benefits, promotions, training, and other privileges of employment. The ADA applies to employers having at least fifteen employees.

An individual with a disability is a person who has a physical or mental impairment that substantially limits one or more major life activities. The act also protects individuals who might be perceived as having such an impairment; likewise, individuals who are not perceived as disabled but who have a record of a qualifying impairment are also covered.

A qualified employee or applicant with a disability is an individual who, with or without reasonable accommodation, can perform the essential functions of the job.

Examples of *reasonable accommodations* are:

- making existing facilities used by employees readily accessible to and usable by disabled employees, including the acquisition of equipment or devices;

- job restructuring or modifying work schedules;

- reassignment to a vacant position;

- adjusting or modifying examinations, training materials, or policies; and,

- providing qualified readers for the visually impaired or interpreters for those with hearing or language difficulties.

An employer is not required to provide reasonable accommodations if it would impose an *undue hardship* on the operation of the employer's business. *Undue hardship* under the ADA is defined as an action requiring significant difficulty or expense when considered in light of factors such as an employer's size and financial resources. In particular, an employer is not required to lower the quality of the delivery of its services to make an accommodation.

Under the ADA, there are complex rules that apply to medical examinations and inquiries regarding disabilities, so you should contact an attorney for more information if you plan to make such inquiries or require any physical examination.

IN PLAIN ENGLISH

For more information on the Civil Rights Act, the Equal Pay Act, the ADEA, and the ADA, consult the Equal Employment Opportunity Commission website at **www.eeoc.gov**.

HARASSMENT

One of the legal obligations of all business owners is to create a nondiscriminatory work environment. A policy should be established prohibiting any discriminatory language—for example, ethnic jokes, racial slurs, demeaning or degrading comments regarding a certain gender—or other offensive language or actions.

Sexual harassment is one form of illegal discrimination, although harassment based on race and certain other characteristics also violates the Civil Rights Act. There are two basic types of sexual harassment: *quid pro quo* and *hostile work environment*. *Quid pro quo* refers to either a harasser asking for sexual favors in exchange for some advantage in the workplace or a harasser penalizing another person for rejecting his or her sexual advances. A *hostile environment*, on the other hand, is more generalized in that the harasser creates or permits a hostile work environment through language, activities, or conduct.

An employer is subject to vicarious liability for a hostile work environment. That means the employer will be responsible for the actions and language of a supervisor, coworker, or other employee that results in an employee's injury, harm, or damage. If a supervisor has harassed or permitted harassment of an employee and this situation has led to that employee's termination, relocation, or the like, the employer will be held liable for the discriminatory sexual actions of the supervisor. But such drastic outcomes are not necessary—if an employee endures a condition over a period of time from coworkers or supervisors or any other employee, liability on the part of the employer may exist even with the worker's termination or relocation.

To avoid this type of liability, the employer must exercise reasonable care to prevent and promptly correct any harassment behaviors that are reported or otherwise become known to him or her, and the employee who was harassed must have taken advantage of all preventive programs or policies provided by the employer. There is a host of training and other resources available to business owners. Check with your business attorney or state employment division. Many states have anti-harassment policies that add to an employer's duties. California, for example, requires employers with fifty or more employees to provide certain sexual harassment training and education to supervisory employees (information is available at **www.dfeh.ca.gov**).

EMPLOYEE HANDBOOKS

As previously discussed, your business should have an employee handbook. It should set forth, among other things, your policies on sexual harassment and discrimination, hours of work, as well as security, overtime policies, and other work requirements and policies. The handbook should make it clear that it is not an employment contract, and, in fact, that employment is at will. Confidentiality should also be covered. This document should be drafted or reviewed by a business attorney because there are numerous requirements for legal notices and other information that a layperson or even a handbook software program may fail to properly address.

If you plan to monitor your employee's Internet usage, email, computer files, phone calls, voice mail, and the like; to use video surveillance; or, to conduct searches of employees' personal belongings (such as items in their lockers), you should include a specific written employee privacy policy identifying the types of situations in which employees should not have an expectation of privacy. Note that your employees do have certain privacy rights, such as privacy in the restroom. Any monitoring must be done in a nondiscriminatory manner to ensure quality and equitably enforced policies and standards.

ZERO TOLERANCE POLICIES

A *zero tolerance standard* will best protect an employer from discrimination claims. An employee handbook containing policies against sexual harassment, offensive behaviors, and the like is a good starting point. A well-drafted discrimination policy will apply to behavior and oral and written (including electronic) communications. It will include procedures that provide employees with a way to confidentially report problems regarding offensive or harassing behavior and will direct management on how to investigate and resolve the issues. The process should include an employee appeals procedure for any adverse findings. The complaint and appeals procedures should permit an employee to contact someone other than the employee's immediate supervisor, since that supervisor may be the one responsible for the conduct.

Employees should be advised that both the complaints and the appeals need to be put in writing so that there can be no misunderstandings, although the first step often is oral reporting of the complaint. A well-drafted policy will state that the employer will, whenever possible, provide complaining employees and witnesses reasonable confidentiality, but it should be made clear that there can be no assurance of confidentiality because it may become necessary for management to disclose the identity and testimony of relevant parties as part of its investigation or in a legal proceeding.

FAMILY AND MEDICAL LEAVE ACT

The *Family and Medical Leave Act* (FMLA) provides employees the opportunity to take up to twelve weeks of unpaid, job-protected leave per year. It also requires that their group health care benefits be maintained during the leave. FMLA applies to employees who have worked for the employer for at least twelve months (and 1,250 hours within that twelve-month period) and who meet eligibility requirements. The FMLA must be followed by companies who employee fifty or more employees.

Leave may be given for any of the following reasons:

- for the birth and care of the newborn child of an employee;

- for placement with the employee of a child for adoption or foster care;

- to care for an immediate family member (spouse, child, or parent) with a serious health condition;

- to take medical leave when the employee is unable to work because of a serious health condition; or,

- to take off work due to pregnancy complications.

When the worker returns to the job, the job may be the exact job that the employee left or it may be an equivalent job—with equivalent duties, pay, and benefits. The only employees to whom this act would not apply are *key employees* whose absence from their positions would cause *substantial and grievous economic injury* to the employer.

There are certain notice requirements as well as rules for requiring medical certification of the need for leave. Further information can be found at the U.S. Department of Labor website, **www.dol.gov**. Also, you should consult your attorney as to whether your state maintains a supplemental leave act.

TERMINATION OF EMPLOYMENT

If the individual working for you is an independent contractor or has an employment contract, the contract between you and that person will govern your respective rights of termination. On the other hand, if the individual is an at-will employee, care must be taken not to become responsible for a wrongful termination when dismissing the individual.

Wrongful Termination

Historically, an employee who was not under contract could be terminated for any reason whatsoever. Now an employee's job can be terminated for the right reason or for no reason at all, but cannot be terminated for the wrong reason. For example, one case held that an employee whose employment was terminated for refusing to commit perjury before a legislative committee was entitled to recover against the employer for wrongful termination. The public policy in having individuals testify honestly was considered more important than the employer's right to control the employment relationship.

Courts have become even more protective of the rights of employees. In a 1983 case, *Novosel v. Nationwide Insurance Company*, the U.S. Court of Appeals held that the power to hire and fire could not be used to dictate an employee's political activity, and that even a nongovernmental entity is limited by the Constitution in its power to discharge an employee. The court, in essence, held that one's right to exercise constitutionally protected free speech was more important than the employer's right to control an employee's conduct.

Wrongful termination cases generally fall into certain categories. Employers may not legally terminate an employee's job for:

- refusing to commit an unlawful act, such as committing perjury or refusing to participate in welfare or Medicare fraud;

- performing a public obligation, such as serving on a jury or serving in a military reserve unit;

- exercising a statutory right, such as filing a claim for workers' compensation; or,

■ any reason based on unlawful discrimination (e.g., discrimination based on race, gender, or the like).

Some courts appear to go quite far in holding that an employer cannot discharge an employee unless there is just cause for termination. Some laws contain specific prohibitions in some circumstances on the termination of employees for *whistleblowing*, that is, cases in which employees notify government authorities of wrongful acts by the employer, such as tax evasion, or cases in which employees tell licensing boards about wrongful acts of health care practitioners.

Progressive Discipline

Perhaps an employer who uses evaluations should employ what has been characterized as *progressive discipline*. This procedure is initiated by orally warning a problem employee of your concern and progressively imposing disciplinary practices until termination becomes the only form of recourse left. Care should be taken not to violate the employee's rights since the liability for wrongful termination can be catastrophic to a health care practice. When in doubt, an employer should contact an attorney with some experience in the field of employment relations. In this area, as with many others, preproblem counseling can prevent a good deal of time-consuming and costly litigation.

CHAPTER 5

Contracts

Contracts constitute a fundamental legal and practical problem in virtually every business, including medical, dental, and other health care practices. Clearly, we cannot cover the entire field of contract law, but we can help you become aware of some of the ramifications of contract law and enable you to see where you need protection.

IN PLAIN ENGLISH

A *contract* is a promise or set of promises that the law will enforce as binding on the people or entities that made the promises. A promise can be as simple as, "I promise to sell you a package of cotton balls if you promise to pay me 59¢ for it." If you do not perform your promise, you will be liable for breach of the contract.

The law requires that the parties to a contract perform the promises they have made to each other. In the event of nonperformance—usually called a *breach*—the law provides remedies to the injured party. For the purposes of this discussion, we will assume that the contract is between two people, although it can involve business organizations such as partnerships or professional corporations as well.

The three basic elements of every contract are:

1. the offer;

2. the acceptance; and,

3. the consideration.

For example, suppose a salesperson shows a doctor an ultrasound machine and suggests that she buy it (the offer). The doctor says she likes it and wants it (the acceptance). They agree on a price (the consideration). That is the basic framework, but a great many variations can be played on that theme.

TYPES OF CONTRACTS

Contracts may be express or implied, and they may be oral or written. On this latter point, you should be aware of at least four types of contracts that must be in writing if they are to be legally enforceable:

1. any contract that, by its terms, cannot be completed in less than one year;

2. any contract for the sale of real estate;

3. any contract that involves the sale of goods for over $500; and,

4. any contract in which one party agrees to pay someone else's debts.

IN PLAIN ENGLISH

The law holds you to your word, and the law will enforce oral agreements. Almost any contractual agreement can be made orally. In general, oral agreements are binding, and you can be held liable for failing to perform your part of an oral agreement.

An *express contract* is one in which all the details are spelled out. For example, you might make a contract with a pharmaceutical company for a specific quantity of flu vaccine to be delivered to you on October 1, at a specific price, to be paid for within thirty days of receipt.

That is fairly straightforward. If either party fails to live up to any material part of the contract, a breach has occurred, and the other party may withhold performance of his or her obligation until receiving assurance that the breaching party will perform. In the event no such assurance is forthcoming, the aggrieved party may have a cause of action and go to court for breach of contract.

If the serum is delivered on October 15 and you had scheduled a flu vaccine clinic during the week of October 1 and had notified the supplier of that fact, then time was an important consideration and you would not be required to accept the late shipment. If, however, time was not a material consideration, then even with the slight delay this probably would be considered *substantial performance* and you would have to accept the delivery.

IN PLAIN ENGLISH

The law will not necessarily presume that you needed the goods exactly on the date when delivery was promised or expected, so you should protect yourself by making sure your counterpart knows if a certain date for performance is important to you, and indicate that performance on or before that date is a requirement of the agreement.

The terms the parties expressly agree on make up the *express contractual terms* of their agreement. Express contracts can be either oral or written, although if you are going to the trouble of expressing contractual terms, you should put your understanding in writing. Those terms that you forget to put in the agreement might be covered by the concept of *implied contractual terms*. Implied contractual terms, sometimes referred to as *implied contracts*, are not the opposite of express contracts. Instead, they are a stop-gap function of the law that fills in terms when necessary to complete the transaction or arrangement of the parties when they have left terms out of their agreement, whether oral or in writing, that turn out to be important. A simple example is your calling a supplier to order tongue depressors without making any express statement that you will pay for them. The promise to pay is implied in the order and is enforceable when the product is delivered.

IN PLAIN ENGLISH

The term *implied contract* does not mean accidental contracts that neither party intended to enter into. The term applies to the situation where there is an agreement between two parties, but the parties did not discuss certain terms, such as time or place of delivery. Sometimes, those terms become necessary to determine. In these circumstances, the law inserts certain baseline, common, reasonable terms that will fill in the gap, e.g., a reasonable time and reasonable place for delivery. In essence, the law *implies* that these would have been the terms if the parties had ever talked about these topics. Although the law implies common, reasonable terms, they may not be the ones the parties would have found to be ideal in their situation, so it is always a good idea to think through the entire deal and try to discuss or, better yet, to put into writing all the terms and conditions that you think are important for the deal to work. Lawyers are adept at anticipating terms and conditions that the parties may not have thought of, so it is a good idea to consult an attorney for guidance on your important contractual agreements.

With implied contracts, things can often become a lot stickier. Suppose your staff neglects to obtain a new patient's signature on the appropriate form obligating the patient to pay for services. You fill the patient's cavity. Is there an implied contract to pay in this arrangement? That may depend on whether you are normally in the business of giving away your services.

You enter into many contracts without thinking much about them, such as those exchanges of promises that take place between your practice and the company supplying your telephone service. (The telephone company agrees to provide certain telecommunications services in exchange for your promise to pay for those services under certain agreed-upon terms.) Perhaps the more problematic contracts are those that you enter into on a regular but intermittent basis for the purchase or sale of goods and services critical to the ongoing viability and smooth running of your practice.

UNDERSTANDING CONTRACT PRINCIPLES: OFFER, ACCEPTANCE, AND CONSIDERATION

Let us examine the principles of offer, acceptance, and consideration in the context of several potential situations for a hypothetical practitioner, Dr. Smith. We will look at the following situations and see whether an enforceable contract comes into existence.

Scenario 1: At a cocktail party, Jones expresses an interest in Dr. Smith's services. "I hurt my back tilling the garden," Jones tells Dr. Smith. "I'm going to come by for treatment one of these days."

Is this a contract? If so, what are the terms of the offer—the particular treatment, the specific price? No, this is not really an offer that Dr. Smith can accept. It is nothing more than an opinion or a vague expression of intent.

Scenario 2: Brown offers to pay $100 for two one-hour sessions of acupuncture treatment for her sore back. Dr. Smith's normal fee for two such sessions is $120, but Dr. Smith agrees to accept the lower fee.

Is this an enforceable contract? Yes. Brown has offered, in unambiguous terms, to pay a specific amount for a specific treatment, and Smith has accepted the offer. A binding contract exists.

Scenario 3: One day Olson shows up at Dr. Smith's office for her appointment, sees that Dr. Smith is selling a couch from the waiting room, and offers $200 for it. Dr. Smith accepts and promises to deliver the couch, at which time Olson will pay for it. An hour later, Brown shows up. She likes the couch and offers Dr. Smith $300 for it. Can Dr. Smith accept the later offer?

No. A contract exists with Olson. An offer was made and accepted. The fact that the object has not yet been delivered or paid for does not make the contract any less binding.

Scenario 4: Dr. Smith and Green discuss treating Green's anxiety disorder with herbs and aromatherapy. Green offers to pay Dr. Smith for the treatment if the results are satisfactory to him, but after Dr. Smith treats Green, Green says the results do not satisfy him.

Green is making the offer in this case, but the offer is conditional upon his satisfaction with the treatment. Dr. Smith can only accept the offer by producing something that meets Green's subjective standards—a risky business. There is no enforceable contract for payment until such time as Green indicates that he is satisfied with the results of the treatment.

Scenario 5: Suppose Green is satisfied with the result of the treatment. He comes to Dr. Smith's office and says that the treatments have completely cured his anxiety disorder and he is satisfied with the results, but then when Dr. Smith requests payment, he says he has changed his mind.

That is too late. The contract became binding at the moment Green indicated the treatment to be satisfactory. If Green then refuses to pay, he would be breaching his contract.

ORAL OR WRITTEN CONTRACTS?

Contracts are enforceable only if they can be proven. A great deal of detail often is lost in the course of remembering a conversation. The best practice, of course, is to get it in writing. The function of a written contract is not only that of proof but also to make very clear the understanding of the parties regarding the agreement and the terms of the contract.

Some health care practitioners prefer to do business strictly on the basis of a handshake and a so-called *gentlemen's agreement*, particularly with their immediate suppliers and retailers. The assumption seems to be that the best business relations are those based on mutual trust alone. Although there may be some validity to this, practitioners nevertheless really should put all oral agreements into writing. Far too many trusting people have suffered adverse consequences because of their idealistic reliance on the sanctity of oral contracts.

IN PLAIN ENGLISH
ORAL CONTRACTS: NOT WORTH THE PAPER THEY'RE PRINTED ON?

The knock against oral contracts is not that they are unenforceable, but rather that it is far too easy for two honest, fair-minded, average human beings to forget the content of their conversations and the details of their agreements over even a short period of time. Honest minds can differ as to their recollections of their promises, and differences like these can result in a breakdown in the performance of the agreement. All of these problems can be avoided simply by putting the terms of the agreement in writing.

Under even the best of business relationships, it is still possible that one or both parties might forget the terms of an oral agreement. Or both parties might have quite different perceptions about the precise terms of the agreement reached. When, however, the agreement is put into writing, there is much less doubt as to the terms of the arrangement, although even a written contract may contain ambiguities if it is not drafted with considerable care. Thus a written contract generally functions as a safeguard against subsequent misunderstanding or forgetful minds.

Perhaps the principal problem with oral contracts lies in the fact that they cannot always be proven or enforced. Proof of oral contracts typically centers on the conflicting testimony of the parties involved. And if none of the parties is able to establish by a preponderance of evidence that his or her version of the contract is the correct one, the oral contract may be considered nonexistent—as though it had never been made. The same result might ensue if the parties cannot remember the precise terms of the agreement.

WHEN WRITTEN CONTRACTS ARE REQUIRED

Even if an oral contract is established, it may not always be enforceable. As already noted, there are some agreements that must be in writing in order to be legally enforceable. An early law that was designed to prevent fraud and perjury, known as the *statute of frauds*, provides that any contract that by its terms cannot be fully performed within one year must be in writing. This rule is narrowly interpreted, so if there is any possibility, no matter how remote, that the contract could be fully performed within one year, the contract need not be reduced to writing.

For example, if a physician agreed to provide physical exams to employees of a local business each year for a period of five years, the contract would have to be in writing since by the very terms of the agreement there is no way the contract could be performed within one year. If, on the other hand, the contract called for the physician to perform fifty physicals within a period of five years, the contract would not have to be in writing under the statute of frauds, since it is possible, though perhaps not probable, that the physician would perform all fifty physicals within the first year. The fact that the doctor does not actually complete performance of the contract within one year is immaterial. So long as complete performance within one year is within the realm of possibility, the contract need not be in writing to be enforceable—it may be oral.

The statute of frauds further provides that any contract for the sale of goods valued at $500 or more is not enforceable unless it has been put into writing and signed by the party against whom enforcement is being sought. The fact that a contract for a price in excess of $500 is not in writing does not void the agreement or render it illegal. The parties are free to perform the oral arrangement, but, if one party refuses to perform, the other will be unable to legally enforce the agreement.

The law defines goods as all things that are movable at the time of making the contract except for the money used as payment. The real question becomes whether a particular contract involves the sale of goods for a price of $500 or more. Although the answer would generally seem to be fairly clear, ambiguities may arise.

For example, if a supplier agrees to provide a practice with all its pharmaceutical needs for the coming year, how is the price to be determined? Or if the pharmaceutical company sells a variety of items to a doctor where the total purchase price exceeds $500 but the price of an individual item is less than $500, which price governs? In light of these possible ambiguities, the safest course is to put all oral contracts into writing.

CONTRACTS WITH BUSINESSES

It should be noted that when business organizations are involved, there are additional considerations, such as whether the person acting on behalf of the business has appropriate authority, how that authority must be evidenced, and regardless of authority, whether that individual's act will be deemed within the appropriate scope of the business. Most of the time these issues never appear on the radar screen; we talk to the right people, bargain with the right people, and make binding agreements with the right people at the organization who have the proper authority to make binding agreements on behalf of the business. Normally, a business wants to put the right people in touch with you because making proper contracts simply is good business. But once in a while, you will find yourself in a situation where it is not entirely clear whether or not the person you are dealing with is properly empowered to make the promises that are necessary for the negotiations. These issues complicate the contracting process and affect both the analysis and enforcement of contracts that may have been entered into in less than optimal circumstances because of the authority of the persons who did the negotiation.

If you have any suspicions regarding the authority or propriety of the actions of a person dealing with you on behalf of a company or other business organization, you should discuss your concerns with an attorney. You also are free to ask to speak to higher management at the organization to confirm the actual authority of the person you are dealing with. It is not enough for the persons you are dealing with to give you assurances that they have the proper authority. You must receive the assurances from a senior officer of the business who is authorized to speak on behalf of the business.

JUDGING THE COST OF WRITTEN AGREEMENTS

At this point, health care practitioners might object to the advice given here, asserting that they do not have the time, energy, or patience to draft contracts. After all, they are in business to provide health care services, not to formulate written contracts steeped in legal jargon. Fortunately, you will not always be required to do this, since the supplier will generally have a satisfactory contract in the form of an invoice. Simple invoices listing items, prices, and delivery terms are fine, but be wary of forms that have multiple additional provisions (most likely appearing in tiny print) because these form contracts will almost invariably be one-sided with all terms in favor of whoever paid to have them drafted.

As an alternative, you could employ an attorney to draft contracts, but this might be cost-effective only for substantial transactions; for example, the lease for your premises; employment contracts with your staff; contracts for the purchase or sale of a practice, including a sale to a hospital; long-term contracts for the supply of large quantities of pharmaceuticals or other supplies on a regular or as-needed basis; or, contracts with third-party payors such as insurance companies. In these situations you should retain an attorney who is experienced in real estate law or commercial law relating to health care businesses and practices. With respect to smaller transactions, the legal fees may be much larger than the benefits derived from having a written contract.

UCC CONFIRMING MEMORANDUM

The *Uniform Commercial Code* (UCC), a compilation of commercial laws enacted, at least in part, in every state, provides practices with a third and perhaps the best alternative. You need not draft contracts or rely on anyone else (a supplier, retailer, or attorney) to do so. The UCC provides that where both parties are merchants and one party sends to the other a written confirmation of an oral contract within a reasonable time after that contract was made, and the recipient does not object to the confirming memorandum within ten days of its receipt, the contract will be deemed enforceable.

It should be emphasized that the sole effect of the *confirming memorandum* is that neither party can use the statute of frauds as a defense, assuming that the recipient fails to object within ten days after receipt. The party sending the confirming memorandum must still prove that an oral contract was, in fact, made prior to or at the same time as the written confirmation. But once such proof is established, neither party can raise the statute of frauds to avoid enforcement of agreement.

IN PLAIN ENGLISH

A *merchant* under the Uniform Commercial Code (UCC) is defined as any person who normally deals in goods of the kind sold or who, because of occupation, represents herself or himself as having knowledge or skills peculiar to the practices or goods involved in the transaction. Most businesspeople who buy or sell goods for their business will be considered merchants for purposes of the UCC.

The advantage of the confirming memorandum over a written contract lies in the fact that the confirming memorandum can be used without the active participation of the other contracting party. It would suffice, for example, to simply state: "This memorandum is to confirm our oral agreement."

But since you still would have to prove the terms of that agreement, it would be useful to provide a bit more detail in the confirming memorandum, such as the subject of the contract, the date it was made, and the price or other consideration to be paid. Thus you might draft something like the following.

> *This memorandum is to confirm our oral agreement made on July 3, 2008, pursuant to which supplier agreed to deliver to purchaser on or before September 19, 2008, 5,000 cotton balls for the purchase price of $50.*

The advantages of providing some detail in the confirming memorandum are twofold. First, in the event of a dispute, you could introduce the memorandum as proof of the terms of the oral agreement. And second, if the recipient does not object to what you state in the memorandum, the recipient of the memorandum will be precluded from offering any proof regarding the terms of the oral contract that contradicts the terms contained in the memorandum.

IN PLAIN ENGLISH

If drafting a complete written contract proves too burdensome or too costly, the health care practitioner should submit a memorandum in confirmation of the oral contract. This at least surpasses the initial barrier raised by the statute of frauds, and by recounting the terms of the agreement in the memorandum, the practitioner is in a much better position to prove the terms of the oral contract at a later date.

If there is no response or rebuttal given to the memorandum, the recipient or, for that matter, party sending the memorandum can introduce proof only regarding terms of the oral contract that are consistent with the terms, if any, found in the memorandum. Thus the purchaser in the previous example would be precluded from claiming that the contract called for delivery of ten thousand cotton balls because the quantity was stated in the written memo and not objected to. On the other hand, the purchaser would be permitted to testify that the oral contract required the supplier to use sterile cotton balls since this testimony would not be inconsistent with the terms stated in the memorandum.

ADDITIONAL TERMS

One party to a contract can prevent the other from adding or inventing terms that are not spelled out in the confirming memorandum by ending the memorandum with a clause requiring all other provisions to be contained in a written and signed document. Such a clause might read:

> *This is the entire agreement between the parties and no modification, alteration, or additional terms shall be enforceable unless in writing and signed by both parties.*

If you use such a clause, be sure there are no additional agreed-to terms that have not been included in the written document. A court generally will be confined to the four corners of the document when trying to determine what was agreed to by the parties. This means that nothing more than what is on the paper containing the agreement will be allowed as evidence.

An exception to this rule is that a court may allow oral evidence for the purpose of interpreting ambiguities or explaining the meaning of certain technical terms in the agreement. The court may also permit the parties to introduce evidence of past practices in connection with the contract in the dispute, in connection with other contracts between the parties, or even in connection with contracts between one of the parties and other entities not a party to the contract in dispute.

To sum up, health care professionals should not rely on oral contracts alone since they offer little protection in the event of a dispute. The best protection is afforded by a written contract. In some instances, the maxim that oral contracts are not worth the paper they are printed on rings true.

SUMMARY OF ESSENTIALS TO PUT IN WRITING

A contract rarely need be—or should be—a long, complicated document written in legal jargon designed to provide a handsome income to lawyers. Indeed, a contract should be written in simple language that both parties can understand and should spell out the terms of the agreement.

A typical contract would include:

- the date of the agreement;

- identification of the two parties—the buyer and seller, in the case of sale of goods or services;

- a description of the goods or services to be sold or provided;

- the price or other consideration; and,

- the signatures of the parties involved.

To supplement these basics, the agreement should spell out whatever other terms might be applicable: time and place of performance, pricing arrangements, payment schedules, insurance coverage, liability apportionment, and so forth.

Finally, it should be noted that a written document that leaves out essential terms of the contract presents many of the same problems of proof and ambiguity as an oral contract. Contract terms should be well-conceived, clearly drafted, conspicuous (i.e., not in tiny print that no one can read), and in plain English so everyone understands what the terms of the contract are.

CHAPTER 6

Borrowing from Banks

Commercial loans can be a valuable source of needed capital for health care professionals. Because lending policies vary dramatically from institution to institution, you should talk to several banks to determine which might be likely to lend to your business and which have the most favorable loan terms. While lenders by nature are conservative in their lending policies, you may discover some to be more flexible than others.

To save time and increase the chances of loan approval, it makes sense to approach first those banks that are most likely to view your proposal favorably and whose lending criteria you feel you can meet. Your search for a loan should not be limited to your community. A statewide, regional, or even national search may be necessary before you find the right combination of willing lender and favorable terms.

IN PLAIN ENGLISH

Using your credit card as a source of financing is not a good idea except in the most extreme of circumstances. Interest rates are high and the terms are usually not favorable for business planning. You must, generally, also personally guarantee any business credit card debt. As a short-term source that you can pay off in a month or two, credit cards might be used as a stop-gap cash flow tool, but proper business management would call for a line of credit or other loan device.

Note that while interest rates are important, they should not be your only concern when choosing a lender. There may be other benefits to working with a lender who does not offer the lowest rate.

After having shopped the marketplace and having decided on a particular bank, you will be ready for the next step—preparing the loan proposal. The importance of being properly prepared before taking this critical step cannot be overemphasized. Loan officers are not likely to be impressed by a hastily prepared application containing vague, incomplete information and unsubstantiated claims. Many loan requests are doomed at this early stage because ill-prepared applicants fail to adequately present themselves and their practice to the lender, even though the proposed ventures are, in fact, sound.

Be sure to submit applications only for credit that you believe your practice needs, only after adequate preparation, and only to lenders you believe are likely to actually make the loan, since credit applications can lower the credit rating of the person or entity making the application.

THE LOAN PROPOSAL

Inexperience with the bank's lending procedures can result in an unexpected rejection. Knowing the bank's lending policy and following its procedure is, therefore, essential. At a minimum, a borrower should be prepared to satisfactorily address each of the following questions.

- Is your practice creditworthy?

- Do you need a short-term (one year or less) or long-term (more than one year) loan?

- For what purpose do you need the loan?

- How much money do you really need?

- What kind of collateral do you and your practice have to secure the loan?

- What are the lender's rules, and what limitations would apply to this loan?

The lender's decision to grant or refuse the loan request will be based on your answers to these questions. It is ironic that the health care practices most likely to qualify for a loan are those that do not need the loan—they are well-run, profitable ventures that have no cash-flow problems and generate lots of income. But with attention to these factors even a practice that desperately needs a loan can prepare an application that will be granted.

IS YOUR PRACTICE CREDITWORTHY?

The ability to obtain money when you need it may be as important to the operation of your practice as having a good location and the right equipment. But before an institution will agree to lend you money, the loan officer must be satisfied that you and your business constitute a good risk—that is, that you are creditworthy. This decision will include the following considerations.

Do You Have a Good Reputation?

The lender will want to know what sort of person you are. Do you have a good reputation in the community and in your profession? Are you known in the community? What is your past credit history, and what is the likelihood that you will repay the loan if your practice falters or even fails?

Despite its subjective nature, this character factor figures prominently in the lender's decision making. It is not uncommon for a loan officer to deny a loan request, regardless of how qualified the applicant appears on paper, if the officer is not convinced of the borrower's good character. The applicant's character will affect the institution's decisions on well-collateralized loans, as well as on *signature loans*, which require only the applicant's signature and are available only to those with the highest credit standing, business integrity, and management skills.

For What Purpose Is the Money Needed?

Your lender will want to know if the money is needed to cover a cash flow problem, to purchase supplies such as drugs, or to acquire fixed assets such as medical equipment. The answer to this inquiry will determine what type of loan—long-term or short-term—the applicant should request. Loans needed to cover a cash flow problem or for inventory generally will be short-term loans requiring repayment within one year or less. This is because the bank will likely anticipate repayment from the collection of your accounts receivable.

Intermediate-term loans, requiring payment between one and five years, and long-term loans, which are those extending payments over ten or even fifteen years, are more appropriate for purchases of fixed assets, since repayment is expected to be made not from the sale of these assets, but from the earnings generated by your ongoing use of them. Those assets produce income at a much slower rate, hence the bank's willingness to allow repayment over a longer period. Bear in mind that commercial lenders are interested in offering funds to successful businesses in need of additional capital to expand and increase profitability. They are not as inclined to make loans to businesses needing the money to pay off existing debts.

When and How Will the Loan Be Repaid?

When and how the loan will be repaid is closely associated with the preceding questions of how much money is needed and for what purpose. The banker will now use judgment and professional experience to assess your business ability and the likelihood of your future success. The banker will want to know whether the proposed use of the borrowed funds justifies the repayment schedule requested. You as the borrower must be able to demonstrate that the cash flow anticipated from the proceeds of the loan will be adequate to meet the repayment terms if the loan is granted.

Is the Cushion on the Loan Large Enough?

The lender will want to know if the borrower has included in the loan request a suitable allowance for unexpected developments. That is, does the loan proposal realistically allow for the vicissitudes of operating a health care practice and provide for alternative resources to meet the borrower's obligation if the business expectations are not met? Or is the borrower stretching to the limit, leaving no margin for error, so that repayment can be made only if the proposal is successful? In the latter circumstance, the lender may consider the loan too risky.

IN PLAIN ENGLISH

If the borrower is stretching the limit and leaving no margin for error so that repayment can be made only if the proposed venture is successful, the lender may consider the loan to be too risky.

The Business Outlook

The lender will be evaluating the business outlook for your practice in particular, and for your type of practice in general, in light of contemporary economic realities. Can your proposed use of the loan be reasonably expected to produce the anticipated increased revenues for your practice? While your proposed plan may appear viable on paper, it may not be realistic given the state of the economy within which you operate.

Financial Evidence

Remember that bankers prefer to make loans to solvent, profitable, growing ventures. They seek assurance that the loan will contribute to that growth since your repayment ability is directly related to your success. As noted previously, bankers are generally not interested in lending money so that a practice can pay off already existing loans. To aid the bank in understanding the financial health of your practice, you will probably be asked to provide specific financial data. Two basic financial documents are customarily submitted for this purpose: the *balance sheet* and the *profit and loss statement*. The balance sheet will aid the bank in evaluating your practice's solvency, while the profit and loss statement summarizes its current performance. Unless yours is a new practice, you should be prepared to submit these financial reports for at least the past two or three years, since they are the principal means for measuring your stability and growth potential. Ideally, these statements will have been prepared by an independent certified public accountant (CPA).

ANALYZING YOUR PRACTICE'S POTENTIAL

When interviewing loan applicants and studying the financial records of their businesses, the bank is especially interested in the following facts and figures.

General Information

Are the books and financial records up to date, accurate, and in good condition, or are they incomplete, infrequently maintained, and in disarray? Haphazard record keeping not only fails to reflect the practice's true financial state, but also demonstrates poor managerial skills. For obvious reasons, banks are reluctant to back poorly run businesses, viewing them as too risky.

The lender will also be interested in the current condition of your accounts payable and notes payable. Are those obligations being paid in a timely fashion, or are they overdue? If you are not presently able to meet existing debts, the lender will be hard-pressed to understand how you expect to be able to meet any additional obligations. Perhaps the requested funds will solve cash flow problems you now have and will also increase earnings so that you will be able to bring past-due accounts current while adequately handling the added debt. In this situation, you might overcome the lender's skepticism by presenting a well-thought-out, solid business plan that clearly demonstrates how the new loan will solve, rather than add to, the practice's financial problems and will boost revenues.

Additionally, the lender will likely want to know your salary or draw as well as other employees' salaries to see if they are reasonable. Excessive salaries represent an unacceptable drain on the practice's resources and profits, which may adversely affect the ability to meet debt obligations.

The lender will also be interested in the size of your workforce. Does it seem adequate to maximize the practice's potential, or does it seem excessive compared to other, similar practices? You should be prepared to discuss the adequacy of your insurance coverage and your present tax situation, that is, whether all taxes are paid current.

All of these factors say something about the financial state of your practice. Although the lender may inquire into other areas, the borrower who knows the type of information of interest to a lender, and who can present this information articulately, significantly increases the chances of having the loan approved.

Accounts Receivable

Of particular interest to the bank will be the number of patients that are behind in their payments to you and how far behind they are. The lender also will want to know what percentage of your total accounts receivable is owed by patients who are currently behind in their payments, as well as information on the number of patients with appropriate insurance. The accounts receivable situation is of special interest to a lender when the borrower is relying on those accounts to provide the cash flow needed to service the requested loan.

You also should expect the potential lender to ask if your practice has an adequate cash reserve to cover questionable accounts and whether the accounts receivable have already been pledged as collateral. A lender who secures a loan with collateral that has already been pledged to a prior lender will, in most cases, be limited in its ability to foreclose on that collateral if the debtor defaults. The prior lender has first right to liquidate the collateral, while subsequent lenders will receive only those proceeds remaining after the prior debt is fully satisfied.

Fixed Assets

Since fixed assets can be used to secure the loan, the bank will likely be interested in the type, condition, age, and current market value of your equipment, machinery, and other major assets of your office. You should be prepared to explain how these assets have been depreciated, their useful life expectancy, and whether they have been previously mortgaged or pledged as collateral to another lender. In addition, be ready to discuss any need or plans to acquire fixed assets. On the one hand, this need could mean additional debt obligations in the near future; on the other, it could explain and justify your projected growth.

IN PLAIN ENGLISH

Banks are reluctant to loan money to businesses with haphazardly kept records. Make sure yours are up to date, accurate, and in good condition.

OPTIONS FOR OWNERS OF NEW PRACTICES

The preceding discussion applies primarily to loan requests made by established, proven practices. New business loan applicants probably will not be able to supply much of the information described here. While this will not necessarily preclude having a new practitioner's loan approved, it could make its approval more difficult. You should, however, be aware that new business loans constitute only a small percentage of all business loans made.

This reluctance to finance unproven businesses, understandably frustrating to new owners, is consistent with the traditionally conservative nature of banks, which owe a fiduciary duty to their stockholders and depositors to disburse funds in a prudent, responsible manner. In light of the extraordinarily high failure rate of new businesses, compounded by the fact that a new business generally cannot provide adequate financial data to evaluate its potential for success, the lender is hard-pressed to justify making high-risk loans. Even where the new business borrower offers more than adequate collateral to secure the loan, the request may be denied.

Banks are comfortable lending money and earning profits from the interest charged on their loans. They are not comfortable in the role of an involuntary partner in the failing business of a delinquent debtor. Even though banks secure loans with a wide range of collateral, they understandably are not anxious to have to foreclose on that security. They are not in the business of selling medical equipment or supplies, or of trying to collect a delinquent debtor's accounts receivable. Although banks try to protect themselves by lending only a fraction of the collateral's market value, they still may not obtain the full amount that they are owed in a distress sale of that collateral, since this type of sale traditionally attracts bargain hunters who will often buy only at prices well below true market value. With an understanding of these dynamics, a loan applicant can better appreciate a bank's hesitation in approving a loan.

Nonetheless, banks do make some loans to new businesses. The health care professional will need to demonstrate a good reputation for paying debts and offer evidence of business management skills. Perhaps you have firsthand knowledge and expertise in the type of practice you propose to establish as a result of having been previously involved with a similar practice. Emphasize that. In addition, provide a sound business plan to support your projections. You can further improve your chances of obtaining a loan if you have invested your own money in the practice, thus indicating your confidence in its success. Furthermore, you should show, if possible, that the practice has a good debt-equity ratio and that it is not saddled with inordinately high debt.

Even if your loan application is refused at first, it is important to establish a good working relationship with a bank. Any initial business success will impress upon the bank the soundness of your plan, thereby opening the door for future financing should the need arise.

SHORT-TERM OR LONG-TERM FINANCING?

Once the bank has evaluated the creditworthiness of your practice, you should be ready to explain the appropriateness of the kind of loan requested. We briefly mentioned this topic previously, but it deserves some additional attention. It is important to be able to convince the lender that your proposed use of the borrowed money will generate the additional revenue needed to pay the loan during the repayment period. Short-term loans are appropriate for purchasing supplies or facilitating the collection of outstanding accounts receivable. They are expected to be repaid as the supplies are consumed or the accounts are collected. Long-term loans are customarily used to finance the acquisition of fixed assets, which, though they may produce slow earnings initially, are expected to increase earnings in the long run. Depending upon your credit reputation, short-term loans may be available with or without security. It is more likely that long-term loans will require adequate security, often necessitating a pledge of personal and professional assets.

Loans that are characterized as *lines of credit* provide the business with the opportunity to borrow up to a specified amount at any given time. This can be used to facilitate purchases, help pay salaries when the business is experiencing cash flow problems, or meet any other present need for additional cash. A line of credit is typically available on a long-term basis. Many lenders require the line to be paid off at least once a year, even though the money can be borrowed again immediately thereafter. As with other long-term financing, a line of credit most often will require adequate security in the form of collateral.

HOW MUCH MONEY WILL YOU NEED?

The lender also will be concerned that the amount of the loan is adequate, since an undercapitalized practice is more likely to get into financial trouble. Similarly, a lender will be reluctant to approve a loan that is excessive, since the debt service may result in an unnecessarily high cash drain on the practice. After fees and expenses, the borrower should have the amount necessary to accomplish the desired goal with a slight cushion for error and no more.

Estimating the amounts needed to finance building construction, conversion, or expansion—long-term loans—is relatively easy, as is estimating the cost of fixed-asset acquisition. On the other hand, working capital needs—short-term loans—are more difficult to assess and depend on your practice. To plan your working capital requirements, it is important to know the cash flow of your practice, present and anticipated. This involves a projection of all the elements of cash receipts and disbursements at the time they are likely to occur. These figures should be projected on a monthly basis to aid the bank in its evaluation.

WHAT KIND OF COLLATERAL DO LENDERS REQUIRE?

Sometimes loans will be made solely on the borrower's signature. More frequently, banks will require collateral to secure the loan. Acceptable collateral can take a variety of forms. The type and amount of collateral necessary in a given situation will depend on the particular bank's lending policies and the borrower's financial state. In general, banks will accept the following types of collateral as security for a business loan.

Endorsers', Co-makers', or Guarantors' Promises to Pay

You may have to get other people to sign a note in order to bolster your credit. These people—referred to as *sureties*—may cosign your note as endorsers, co-makers, or guarantors. While the law makes some subtle distinctions as to when each of these sureties becomes liable for the borrower's debt, in essence those parties will be expected to pay back the borrowed funds if the borrower fails to do so. The bank may or may not require a surety to pledge his or her own assets as security for his or her promise to pay upon the borrower's default. This will depend, to a great extent, on each surety's own financial situation.

Assignment of Leases

Assigning a lease as a form of security may be appropriate if your lease is assignable. Most are not. If you cannot tell from reading your lease, you should consult an attorney.

Security Interests

Equipment loans may be secured by giving the bank a lien on the equipment you are buying. The amount loaned will likely be less than the purchase price—how much less will be determined by the present and future market value of the equipment and its rate of depreciation. You will be expected to adequately insure the equipment, properly maintain it and protect it from damage.

Real Estate Holdings

You may be able to borrow against the equity in your personal real estate holdings as well as against those of the business. Again, you will likely be required to maintain the property in good condition and carry adequate insurance on the property for the benefit of the lender, at least up to the amount of the loan.

Accounts Receivable

Many banks will lend money secured by your business's accounts receivable. In effect, the bank is relying on your patients' ability to pay you so you can pay off your note obligation to the bank.

Savings Accounts and Life Insurance Policies

Sometimes you may get a loan by assigning your savings account to the lender. The lender will notify the savings account holder of the existence of the debt in order to ensure that the account will not be diminished during the term of the loan. Loans can also be made up to the cash value of a life insurance policy, but you must be prepared to assign the policy to the lender.

Stocks and Bonds

Stocks and bonds may be accepted as collateral for a loan if they are readily marketable. However, banks will likely lend no more than 75% of the market value of a high-grade security. If the value of the securities drops below the lender's required margin, the borrower may be asked to provide additional security for the loan.

THE LOAN APPLICATION

Having targeted your source for funds and analyzed your practice in terms you now know lenders look at, you are ready to develop the loan request. Although most lenders will require the application to include the same standard essential information, they often differ as to the proper format of the application. Some lenders may provide suggested formats; others may require a specific format. The actual content, length, and formality will depend on the lender's familiarity with your practice, the amount of money requested, and the proposed use of the borrowed funds. A simple application form and a conversation may be adequate for your local banker. The start-up practice seeking substantial funds from lenders unfamiliar with it will be required to provide much more extensive documentation, including a detailed plan of the entire practice.

A business loan applicant is typically asked to submit any or all of the following information.

- *Personal financial statements.* These will indicate the personal net worth of the practice's owner(s). This is helpful in evaluating creditworthiness and revealing potential sources of collateral, as well as estimating repayment capabilities.

- *Recent (previous two years) and current tax returns.* Include returns for the individual owner(s) and for the practice.

- *The practice's financial statements.* These, as mentioned previously, ideally should extend back for at least two or three years and should have been prepared and authenticated by an independent CPA. Cash flow statements and profit projections may also be requested by the lender.

- *A business history.* This should include past profit and loss patterns, current debt-equity ratio, current and projected cash flow, and present and projected earnings.

- *A business plan.* This should explain the proposed use of the requested funds and explain how the loan will benefit the practice. The length and content of this plan will vary according to the financial health of the applicant's practice and the amount and type of loan for which applied.

Other documentation may also be requested. The individual lender will be able to indicate what is needed in light of the given circumstances.

WHAT ARE THE LENDER'S RULES AND LIMITATIONS?

Once the loan has been approved in principle, it is likely that the bank will impose certain rules and constraints on you and your business. These serve to protect the lender against unnecessary risk and against the possibility of your engaging in poor management practices. You, your attorney, and your business advisor should evaluate all the terms and conditions of the loan in order to determine whether it is acceptable. If the bank's requirements are too onerous, it may be appropriate for you to decline this loan and seek alternative financing. Never agree to restrictions to which you cannot realistically adhere. If, on the other hand, the terms and conditions of the loan are acceptable, even though they are demanding, it may be appropriate to take the loan. In fact, some borrowers view these limitations as an opportunity for improving their own management techniques and business profitability.

IN PLAIN ENGLISH

Especially when making long-term loans, the lender will be interested in the net earning power of the borrowing practice, the capability of its management, the long-range prospects of the practice, and the long-range prospects of the health care specialty in question.

As a result of the bank's scrutiny of your practice, the kinds of limitations imposed will depend to a great extent on the practice itself. If the practice is a good risk, only minimal limitations need be set. A poor risk, of course, should expect greater limitations to be placed on it.

There are three common types of limitations you are likely to encounter:

1. repayment terms;

2. use of pledged security; and,

3. periodic reporting.

Repayment Terms

The bank will want to set a loan repayment schedule that accurately reflects your ability to earn revenues sufficient to meet the proposed obligation. Risky businesses can expect shorter terms, while proven enterprises may receive longer periods within which to repay the loan. In addition, the interest rate may also vary depending on the risk quality of the borrower.

Use of Pledged Security

Once a lender agrees to accept collateral to secure a loan, it will understandably be keenly interested in your assurance that, should the need arise, the collateral will still be available to satisfy the debt. To this end, the lender may take actual possession of the collateral if it is stocks, bonds, or other negotiable instruments. Of course, a bank is not likely to take physical possession of a practice's fixed assets, such as X-ray machines, and remove them to the bank's vault. There are, however, other ways by which a bank can obtain possession of your fixed assets while allowing you to use them. For example, the lender could *perfect*—that is, legally establish—a security interest in equipment used in your practice by filing a financing statement in the appropriate state or county office. (*Security interest* is the legal term for a lender's rights in collateral.) Real estate mortgages are perfected by having them recorded in the appropriate government offices. In these situations, the bank may impose restrictions on the use of the collateral and require that it be properly maintained and adequately insured. The bank may further limit or prohibit you from pledging the same collateral for any other business debts or loans.

While this may sound reasonable, you should recognize that such restrictions could seriously hamper your ability to borrow additional funds if the need arises at a future time. For example, where equipment is used as collateral, you must find out exactly how much of your equipment is involved. A bank may ask for only a portion of the equipment to secure the loan. More likely, though, the bank's security interest will extend to all the company's equipment on hand at any given time, including any subsequently acquired equipment. Here lies the potential problem— the equipment's value may well exceed the amount of the loan that it secures. Nonetheless, you may find yourself in the position of not being able to use any of the equipment as collateral for any additional loans. In cases where this situation is likely to arise, you are well-advised to consider alternative sources of collateral.

Periodic Reporting

To protect itself, a lender may require you to supply it with certain financial statements on a regular basis, perhaps quarterly or even monthly. From these statements, the lender can see if the business is, in fact, performing up to the expectations projected in the loan application. This type of monitoring serves not only to reassure the lender that the loan will be repaid, but also to identify and help solve problems before they become insurmountable, and thus threaten the practice's continued viability.

DETAILS OF THE AGREEMENT

The loan agreement itself is a tailor-made document—a contract between the lender and borrower—that spells out in detail all the terms and conditions of the loan. The actual restrictions placed on the loan likely will be found in the agreement under a section entitled "Covenants." *Negative covenants* are things that you may not do without the lender's prior approval, such as incurring additional debt or pledging the loan's collateral or other business assets to another lender as collateral for a second loan. On the other hand, *positive covenants* spell out those things that you must do, such as carry adequate insurance, provide specified financial reports, and repay the loan according to the terms of the loan agreement. Note that—with the lender's prior consent—the terms and conditions contained in the loan agreement can be amended, adjusted, or even waived. Remember, you can often negotiate the loan terms with the lender before signing.

THE IMPORTANCE OF COMMUNICATION WHEN PROBLEMS ARISE

Once a loan is approved and disbursed, the borrower must address a new set of obligations and liabilities. Of course, if all goes according to plan, the loan proceeds are invested, the practice prospers, the loan is repaid on schedule, and all parties live happily ever after. However, the business world is fraught with uncertainty. If the practice falters and revenues tumble, the borrower may not be able to meet the debt obligations. In this unfortunate event, it becomes imperative that the borrower react responsibly, viewing the lender as a potential ally in solving problems, rather than as an adversary.

At least initially, bankers are not eager to exercise their right to foreclose on the collateral securing the loan at the first indication that the debt may not be repaid. They likely have no experience in marketing the types of collateral involved, nor do they want to run a distress sale, which, at best, would probably bring in only a fraction of the money owed. Additionally, foreclosing against the practice's assets further decreases the bank's chance of recovering any of the unpaid balance, since the borrower, having been stripped of the means to carry on the practice, is likely to be insolvent and facing bankruptcy. Even if the lender can liquidate the collateral at its current fair market value, that value may be well below the value agreed upon when the loan was made. For these and other reasons, banks foreclose on collateral only as a last resort.

Bear in mind that, in general, lenders prefer to work with a potentially defaulting debtor to help ease the debt burden so that the borrower can overcome the problems, stay in business, and reestablish the practice's profitability. To this end, lenders, through experience, have learned to identify a variety of red flags as indications that the debtor is experiencing financial difficulty. For example, the alert is sounded when loan payments start to be made later and later each month, or when the practice's account increasingly shows checks being dishonored for insufficient funds.

When the lender sees these signals, the account may be assigned to a separate department set up within the bank to assist borrowers in overcoming problems. The bank may be willing to offer a variety of accommodations to help the borrower: repayment terms can be extended, the amount of payment due each month can be temporarily reduced, or the bank may accept repayment of interest only, until the practice has overcome its temporary difficulties. The bank may be in a position to offer advice for ways to help solve the practice's problems, particularly where poor management is the source of the difficulties.

How far and to what extent the bank will be willing to accommodate a delinquent debtor very often depends on the debtor's attitude and degree of cooperation. Hard-pressed debtors often fail to understand the importance of establishing a cooperative, rather than adversarial, relationship with the lender. At the first sign of trouble, the borrower should take the initiative to notify the bank and explain what is being done to remedy the situation. Expecting a bank to be sympathetic to one's plight and make concessions seems unreasonable in cases where the borrower waits until the debt is long past due before approaching the lender to explain the problems. Nor is a bank likely to be sympathetic toward a borrower who fails to return phone calls and virtually disappears, always unavailable to discuss the problem with the bank.

The lender is likely to be most cooperative with a debtor who alerts the bank to the problems early on, explains what efforts are being made to remedy them, and keeps in close contact with the bank, informing it of current developments and of the progress made toward solving the problems.

A favorably impressed lender can be an invaluable asset to your business, not only in granting loans but also in helping you out in difficult times. Do not underestimate the need for establishing a solid professional relationship with your lender. The ultimate success and growth of your practice may well depend on it.

While our discussion in this chapter has focused on arrangements with banks, there may be other lenders with whom you may desire or need to deal. These might include *factors* (who traditionally have lent medical professionals money against accounts receivable) and other nontraditional lenders who generally charge higher interest rates than banks. You should, of course, discuss any nontraditional arrangement with your attorney before entering into the arrangement.

CHAPTER 7

Collections

If you are fortunate enough to deal with patients who always pay their bills on time, or if you work as an employee, such as for an HMO, the remaining portion of this chapter may be of no interest at all to you. If, however, you have experienced delays in payment or have had some totally uncollectible bills, you should consider the suggestions that follow. There are several ways to deal with collection problems, ranging from preventive action to initiating a lawsuit.

POINT-OF-SALE PAYMENTS

Health care practitioners customarily expect to be paid at the time services are rendered. Such payment is made by the patient using cash, check, credit card, or debit card. It is, therefore, necessary for you to determine whether the cash is authentic, whether the credit card is valid, and whether the check or debit card is going to be honored by the bank. Obviously, the cash sale is the safest way, although you should be aware that counterfeiting is not a thing of the past.

Many patients are covered by insurance, and payment for services rendered to them may come directly from the insurance carrier. Unfortunately, some insurers pay the patient rather than the health care provider. In addition, the insurer may cover only a portion of the charge based on a schedule, or may deny any payment. It is essential for you to require the patient to assume responsibility for any portion of the services not covered by the insurer. If your services are covered by the insurer, you may not collect from the patient except for copayments, deductibles, or any unscheduled services. It is, however, important for you to learn appropriate coding requirements and follow all other requirements of each insurance company.

CASH

Identifying counterfeit cash can be very technical and difficult. Modern scanners and high-quality color printers used by counterfeiters have made it all the more difficult to detect a fake bill. Recently the federal government has moved to the use of watermarks, microprinting, and color-shifting inks, as well as inserted bands in the fabric of the bill showing the denomination in order to thwart modern counterfeiting technology. Occasionally, however, it is simple to detect a fake if the counterfeiter has made a glaring error, such as using George Washington on a five-dollar bill. The federal government is quite diligent in alerting businesspeople to the presence of counterfeit currency in a particular area when it is aware of the problem. The best way to avoid being stuck with a counterfeit bill is to keep your eyes and fingertips open and alert: does the bill look funny or even feel funny? (The proper linen and cotton fabric used to make the bills is a closely guarded commodity, and fake bills generally do not feel like real bills.) In any event, it is a good idea not to accept anything larger than a fifty-dollar bill.

CREDIT CARDS AND DEBIT CARDS

With regard to credit card and debit card fraud, the first thing to do is to compare the signature on the back of the card with the signature on the credit card slip. It is also a good idea to ask to see some form of photo identification to verify that you are dealing with the actual card owner, though this is far from foolproof because identity theft is rampant and experienced thieves will have a fake ID ready. Even more important is to follow the credit card company's procedures carefully. If the company requires you to get authorization for all credit card sales over fifty dollars, then be sure to get that authorization. It may seem time-consuming and troublesome, but the rules are based on bitter experience. If you have made a credit card sale without following the instructions and the credit card turns out to have been stolen or the patient has exceeded his or her credit limit, you are likely to be stuck with the loss.

You should be very careful about taking credit card numbers over the telephone. Take only numbers of individuals that you know. Ask if the card has a security code on the reverse (usually a three-digit number) in addition to getting the card number and expiration date. You should also get the billing address for the card, including the zip code. These steps will help you avoid being defrauded by someone with a stolen card number.

PERSONAL CHECKS

The most frequent payment problems occur over personal checks. A host of things can prevent a check from being honored or cashed by a bank. To begin with, the person who writes the check may be an imposter using a checkbook that actually belongs to someone else. In order to reduce the likelihood of this occurring, you should insist upon seeing at least two pieces of identification, one of which should, ideally, contain a photograph of the person. A current credit card or a check guarantee card with a photograph and signature facsimile or any other photo ID should serve this purpose. Do not accept as identification such items as Social Security cards, library cards, or any other ID that can easily be obtained or forged.

Watch while the person signs the check (otherwise, the signature may have been previously traced from a valid signature) and compare the signature with that of the other identification. While only an expert can identify a good forgery, most people can recognize a clumsy attempt by an amateur.

Accept checks only if they are made out to you and only if they are written for the exact amount of the services. In other words, do not take checks made out to someone else and endorsed to you, and never cash a check or take checks for more than the amount due—that is, when you then have to give change in cash.

Even if the individual writing the check is legitimate, there still are more potential problems. One of the most common difficulties is the problem of insufficient funds to cover the check. If the amount of your bill is substantial, you might wish to request a certified or bank-guaranteed check or money order. However, the inconvenience of requiring the patient to have a check certified may interfere with your relationship and thus is not practical in most situations.

If you know the person writing the check, it is less likely that the person will give you a bad check. Even if the patient is a stranger, the risk of receiving a bad check and not being able to locate the patient afterward can be reduced if the patient's address and phone number are printed on the check or if you copy them onto the check from the pieces of identification you requested from the payor. It is a very good idea to copy the information if it differs in any way from the information printed on the check.

Despite all these precautions, some bad checks do slip through. It is a crime in most states to pay for something with a check that the signer knows will be dishonored. A lawsuit can be brought against a patient to recover the amount of the check. If you win such a suit, most states will allow the recovery of reasonable costs of litigation, including the attorney's fees.

IN PLAIN ENGLISH

A check returned for insufficient funds can be redeposited in the hope that the check will be covered the second time through. Some bad checks simply are the result of a miscalculated account balance or of the patient having received and deposited a bad check in his or her own account. It is always a good idea to make a phone call before hiring a collection agency or filing a lawsuit to collect the debt.

WAYS OF ENCOURAGING PAYMENT

While the law provides vehicles for obtaining payment of legal obligations, it is always preferable for businesspeople to establish benefits that encourage debtors to pay their obligations.

Cash Discounts

A simple way to encourage early payment is by offering cash discounts. The offer of a 5% cash discount for an early or even an on-time payment may be all the encouragement some patients need. Others may be earning more than 5% interest on their money, so they would prefer to keep the money and ignore your 5% reward. You will have to consider other options for these recalcitrant debtors.

Charging Interest on Overdue Payments: Pros and Cons

The other option, which can be combined with the incentive of cash discounts, is to charge interest on payments received after the statement due date. For debtors who can pay on time and simply are choosing not to, charging interest on the amount due increases the cost of withholding the money from you, their creditor.

The interest option, however, involves two possible traps. First, many states still have usury laws that limit the percentage of interest that can be charged. A lender who exceeds the legal interest ceiling may find that the entire debt is forfeited, all interest is forfeited, or a usury penalty is imposed.

The second possible problem is the necessity to comply with the federal *Truth in Lending Act* and the various equivalent state laws. The Truth in Lending Act is basically a disclosure law that requires certain terms to be included on any contract or billing if:

1. credit is offered to consumers;

2. credit is offered on a regular basis;

3. the credit is subject to interest or is payable by a written agreement in more than four installments; and,

4. the credit is primarily for personal, family, or household purposes.

The task of compliance is eased by the availability of preprinted forms containing the required disclosures that are available from legal publishers and attorneys.

While many of the required terms may seem inapplicable to a simple transaction, you are well-advised if you want to charge interest to use a form that contains all the disclosures. Even though they may not be required in every case, omitting them when they are required could expose you to significant liability.

WHEN THE PAYMENT NEVER COMES

If neither the carrot nor the stick is effective in obtaining payment, you have several other options.

Do Nothing

The first possibility is to do nothing. If the amount is small enough, you may simply decide not to pursue collection. Needless to say, if this alternative is selected, you should refrain from providing future care to that patient.

Collection Agencies

A second option would be to hire a collection agency to attempt to collect the debt. Collection agencies have become quite common and many health care practitioners have established relationships with these companies. The charge and terms vary from agency to agency. Some merely take a percentage of the recovery (which might be as high as 50% of the recovery), while others will charge a fixed fee or an up-front fee combined with a lower percentage of the recovery. Others may charge a higher percentage if litigation is necessary. Care should be taken to evaluate the methods, skills, and reputations of the various collection agencies you will find listed in the Yellow Pages. Both the creditor (you) and the collection agency are subject to tight federal regulation and, in many states, state regulation regarding debt collection practices. Agencies that commit unlawful debt collection practices can subject you to liability for their wrongful acts.

Lawsuit

A third option is the instigation of a full-scale lawsuit to force payment. In many states, a formal demand is practical only if the outstanding debt is relatively large because an attorney must be hired and will likely be quite expensive, particularly if the case proceeds all the way to trial.

The court fees charged for filing a case in many states exceed $300. The defendant (the debtor) must be personally served with court papers, which costs an additional amount (in the range of $50–$250 for service with no complications) per defendant. The amount depends on the difficulty of the service and the type of process server you choose or are required to use—sheriff's deputies or marshals generally cost less than private investigators and professional process servers.

Lastly, if the case is won and the buyer still refuses to pay, further proceedings must be initiated at additional cost, to *execute*, or force payment, on the judgment received. All in all, on a moderate debt, the expense involved in a civil trial may amount to more than the debt itself.

Small Claims Court

A simpler and less expensive solution on small debts is to bring an action in small claims court. While the rules vary from state to state, all of the systems are geared toward making the process as swift, accessible, and inexpensive as possible. Moreover, most courts have staff members who help guide people through pleading in small claims court.

The major cost savings in a small claims court proceeding results from the fact that attorneys are not customarily permitted in such courts. Unless they represent themselves or a corporation, attorneys generally may not assist with completion of the necessary forms or appear in court. Even in states where attorneys are not specifically barred by statute, the court rules are set up in such a clear, comprehensible way that an attorney usually is not needed.

A small claims action has other advantages over a conventional lawsuit; however, not all actions can be brought in small claims court. As the name implies, only claims for small amounts can be brought. The definition of *small* ranges from maximums of $5,000 or less in many states to $10,000 or less in others. Moreover, only actions seeking monetary damages are appropriate in small claims court; other forms of relief, such as injunction, cannot be granted.

The small claims process is comparatively swift and inexpensive. Filing fees are generally much less than for regular courts. In addition, in most courts, the creditor is not responsible for informing the debtor that a suit has been brought. The clerk of the court customarily mails the notice to the defendant by certified or registered mail. A small fee generally is charged to cover mailing costs.

In some states, the hearing on a small claims action may be held on a weekend or in the evening. The hearing itself is kept simple. The technical rules of evidence and of legal procedure are not followed. The judge simply hears both sides of the case and allows any evidence or the testimony of any witnesses either party has to offer. Jury trials are never permitted in small claims courts, although the defendant desiring a trial by jury may be able to have the case moved to a conventional court.

An action in small claims court has disadvantages, too. First, the judgment often is absolutely binding, meaning neither party may appeal. Second, the judgment may be uncollectible. In many states, the usual methods of enforcing a judgment— garnishment of wages or liens against property—are unavailable to the holder of a judgment from small claims court. Some jurisdictions permit a small claims court judgment to be converted into a traditional judgment, but this often requires the assistance of an attorney.

For the most part, care in selecting those with whom you do business will minimize the need to use legal means to collect payment for services. If, however, all other methods fail, small claims court is by far the least expensive and easiest way to obtain legal redress for a small outstanding debt.

BANKRUPTCY

When a bankruptcy petition is filed, the debtor is responsible for filing an accurate list of creditors with the bankruptcy court. The court sends a notice of the filing to the listed creditors and gives additional notices to all parties with claims against the bankrupt debtor who are listed with the court or who make an appearance in the case. Even if the amount at stake in the bankruptcy is small, and it seems that it may not be economically practical to pursue the matter, you should file a claim if the court gives notice to do so. Many creditors fail to file claims, often increasing the payment to those who do.

There are two general categories of bankruptcy.

Liquidation Bankruptcy or Straight Bankruptcy

The first category, *liquidation bankruptcy*, referred to as *straight bankruptcy* in Chapter 7 of the Bankruptcy Code, contemplates the prompt conversion of all of the bankrupt's nonexempt property to cash and the payment of creditors to the greatest extent possible. This applies to businesses and individuals. The Bankruptcy Code establishes a pecking order of creditors, giving certain creditors priority for payment. Such creditors would be the U.S. government for taxes and secured parties for the amount of their security interests. Each category of creditor must be paid in full before a lower-priority creditor may be paid at all. If there are insufficient funds to satisfy all creditors in a particular class, the members of that group will receive a pro rata portion of their claim.

Not all of the bankrupt's assets are available for creditors. There are some things that may be retained, such as a modest house, books or tools used in trade, a holy book, clothing, and the like, even after bankruptcy. The list of exempt property varies from state to state and there are federal exemptions, too. In some states, the bankrupt debtor can choose whether to use the state or the federal exemptions.

After the bankrupt's nonexempt assets are completely distributed, the court-appointed trustee will apply to the bankruptcy judge for a discharge order. If the bankrupt has fulfilled all the requirements of the Bankruptcy Code and the judge is satisfied with the proceeding, the bankrupt's debts will be wiped out—all claims against the debtor are discharged—and the proceeding will end. Certain claims, however, cannot be discharged in bankruptcy; for example, any creditor who was not notified of the bankruptcy and given a chance to participate in the proceeding will have a claim that remains viable even after the bankruptcy proceeding has ended. Other claims are not discharged even if the creditor does nothing, such as certain categories of tax debts and child or spousal support obligations.

Reorganization or Work-Out Bankruptcy

The second type of bankruptcy proceeding is the so-called Chapter 11 (for businesses) or Chapter 13 (for individuals) bankruptcy, which refers to a *reorganization* or *work-out* of the debt situation. This follows a somewhat different process than a straight Chapter 7 liquidation bankruptcy. Rather than terminating the business or liquidating all of an individual's assets, a Chapter 11 or Chapter 13 bankruptcy is designed to facilitate an orderly payment to creditors so that the business may survive.

When a Chapter 11 petition is filed and the creditors meet, a reorganization plan is proposed. All legal proceedings for debt collection other than the bankruptcy proceeding are frozen, and the bankrupt is given an opportunity to satisfy the creditors in a timely fashion. Once a plan acceptable to all creditors is prepared, it is presented to the bankruptcy judge. If it is determined that the Chapter 11 reorganization plan is fair and equitable, the judge will approve it and it will be implemented.

A similar process occurs with individual debtors under Chapter 13. A plan is proposed in which the debtor retains a portion of his or her income to meet ordinary and necessary living expenses, and the rest is transferred to a trustee for ultimate distribution to creditors.

Creditors customarily receive more under Chapter 11 or 13 than they do under straight bankruptcy, although reorganization is feasible only for a healthy business suffering a temporary economic reversal or an individual with a job and decent prospects for a continuing income stream. Creditors who have a secured position, such as those who have filed Uniform Commercial Code (UCC) documents to establish their security interest, participate in drafting the Chapter 11 plan. Generally, these creditors would be those who sold on consignment or those who retain a security interest for the purchase price of some merchandise or equipment. A plan will be deemed fair and equitable to the secured creditors, and they may be forced to agree to it, if it provides that they will do the following:

- retain their liens and receive future cash payments equal to the value of the security;

- retain a lien on the proceeds from the sale of their collateral; or,

- receive the equivalent of their interests, such as cash up front or substituted collateral.

In a Chapter 11 proceeding, a secured creditor, in order to have the plan accepted by all the creditors, may be forced to accept a less favorable position than the UCC would allow. Even though that may happen on occasion, someone with a security interest is still far better off than one who is unsecured.

In 2005, Congress enacted significant revisions to the Bankruptcy Code, including adding a means test limiting eligibility for bankruptcy protection under Chapter 7 of the Code, modifying exemptions and restrictions on discharge, and reducing the ability of individuals to file Chapter 7 bankruptcies to discharge their debts. The most commonly noted effect of the revisions has been to drive up the cost of attorney's fees associated with filing for bankruptcy due to the more arduous and time-consuming process involved.

IN PLAIN ENGLISH

Common sense, diligence, and attention to detail are always important attributes for any health care professional. When the economy is weak and money is tight, these attributes are essential. There will probably always be some uncollectible bills, but with proper care and some preventive attention, you can keep these to a minimum.

CHAPTER 8

Renting Your Office

At some point in the life of your practice, you will probably find it necessary to evaluate the terms and conditions of a commercial lease. These are much more subject to negotiation and pitfalls than residential leases, which are tightly regulated in most states. Landlords of commercial properties most likely will retain the services of a real estate broker if not a lawyer for their rental business. As a result, you should consult an attorney with experience in negotiating commercial leases before signing one or, at the very least, you should consider consulting a real estate broker who is experienced in commercial leasing. This discussion is intended to alert you to some of the topics that should arise in your discussion with your lawyer or real estate broker.

IN PLAIN ENGLISH

Even though a commercial lease may look readable and understandable on its face, the terms and conditions are much more subject to negotiation than the terms of a residential lease, and any lease document offered by your landlord is virtually guaranteed to be drafted in a way that overwhelmingly favors the landlord. If you have your own lawyer simply read over the lease, this will allow you to find out the true legal ramifications of certain clauses drafted by the landlord. Having the lawyer negotiate on your behalf will often level the playing field of the landlord and commercial tenant even further.

PREMISES

To begin with, the exact space to be rented should be spelled out in detail in the lease. Determine whether there is a distinction between the space leased and the actual space that is usable. Often, tenants are required to pay rent on commercial space measured from wall to wall (commonly referred to as a *vanilla shell*), even though after the area is built out the resulting usable space may be significantly smaller.

If your space is in a professional building or office complex and you share responsibility for common areas with other tenants, the following responsibilities should be explained.

- Will you be responsible for cleaning and maintaining these areas, or will the landlord?

- When will the common areas be open or closed?

- What other facilities are available to you, such as restrooms, storage areas, and the like?

COST

Another important item is the cost of the space; will you be paying a flat monthly rental or one that will change based on your earnings at the location? In order to evaluate the cost of the space, you should compare it with similar spaces in the same locale. Do not be afraid to negotiate for more favorable terms. Are the *common area maintenance* (CAM) charges billed separately or are they incorporated into the monthly rent?

TERM

It is also important for you to consider the period of the lease. If, for example, you intend to rent only for a year or two, then you are concerned with a short-term lease; however, it is probably still a good idea to get an option to extend. Moving can cause a lot of problems with mail and telephone numbers. Besides, if you move every year or two, some patients may feel that you are unstable, and patients who consult you only sporadically may not know where to find you after the lease period ends. Worse still, they may find a competing health care practitioner in your old space.

RECORDING THE LEASE

Long-term leases are recordable in some states. Recording, where permitted, is generally accomplished by having the lease—or a shorter Memorandum of Lease—filed in the same office as a deed to that property would be filed. Check with a local real estate title company or real estate attorney for the particulars in your state.

IN PLAIN ENGLISH

If you are in a position to record your lease, it is probably a good idea to do so because you will then be entitled to receive legal and other notices that are related to the property.

RESTRICTIONS AND ZONING

It is essential for you to determine whether there are any restrictions on the particular activity you wish to perform on the leased premises. For example, there may be some restrictions on the use of X-ray equipment. Some landlords impose weight restrictions on any equipment installed in the office. Care should be taken not to sign a lease that will restrict you from opening another facility close to the one being rented.

Be sure the lease provides that you are permitted to use any sign or advertising on the premises, or spells out any restrictions. It is not uncommon, for example, for historic landmark laws to regulate signs on old buildings. Can you put a sign in your window or in front of your building? Some zoning laws or sign ordinances prohibit stand-alone commercial signs or signs of a certain size or appearance, or impose requirements for commercial signage such as a monumental installation (brick or concrete design) that is much more expensive to put in place. It is a good idea to insist on a provision that puts the burden of obtaining any required permit or variance on the landlord or, if you are responsible for them, the inability to obtain them should be grounds for terminating the lease without penalty.

The lease should also contain a provision for parking. Will you be provided with adequate spaces for yourself, your employees, and your patients? If there is no dedicated parking lot or garage, check to see that there are an adequate number of spaces on the street during business hours for patients to use.

REMODELING

You should also be aware that extensive remodeling may be necessary for certain spaces to become suitable for your use. If this is the case, it is important for you to determine the extent to which you can remodel the premises and, equally important, who will be responsible for the costs of remodeling. In addition, it is essential to find out whether it will be necessary for you to restore the premises to their original, preremodeled condition when the lease ends. This can be expensive and, in some instances, impossible.

Americans with Disabilities Act

The *Americans with Disabilities Act of 1990* (ADA) affects not only employees (as discussed in Chapter 4) but real estate as well. The ADA requires "places of public accommodation," meaning businesses that are open to the public (including health care facilities), to be reasonably accessible to the disabled. The phrase *reasonably accessible* is not precise, and thus it would benefit you to determine what must be done to fulfill the requirements of this federal statute. Typically, accessibility issues include providing:

- access to wheelchairs in entrances, exits, waiting areas, and restroom facilities;

- bars, rails, and other design elements to accommodate other handicapped usage of facilities and restrooms;

- levered or automatically operated disability-accessible doors, entrances, and elevators; and,

- signs and elevator buttons that are brailled for the visually impaired.

The costs to remodel existing premises to make them ADA compliant may be excessive, so it would be an excellent idea to negotiate who will cover the cost of the necessary changes. The ADA is quite technical and you should consult with your attorney about its requirements before renting or purchasing an office.

Environmental Laws

Environmental laws may prohibit the use of your space for certain activities. It is essential for you to determine whether any of the materials used in your practice will violate federal, state, or local rules with respect to hazardous materials. In addition, there can be hazardous materials cleanup problems resulting from prior uses of the space you will occupy. For example, if your premises were previously used by a dry cleaner, chemical company, or any business that maintained underground storage tanks for oil, gasoline, or other harmful products, this may require an expensive cleanup operation prior to any occupation. Other issues, such as whether your property contains any asbestos, lead-based paint, certain toxic molds, or other harmful substances, may arise before or after you obtain possession of the space. These present specialized problems in the costs of remodeling and occupation. It is essential for you to spell out who will bear the costs of any environmental compliance in the lease.

UTILITIES: WHO PAYS FOR WHAT?

If you need special hookups, such as extra water or electrical lines, you should determine whether the landlord will provide them or whether you have to bear the cost. Of course, if the leased premises already have the necessary facilities, you should question the landlord regarding the cost of these utilities. Are they included in the rent or are they to be paid separately? Are they on a separate meter or will the landlord merely prorate your portion of the utilities?

In some locations, garbage pickup is not a problem, since it is one of the services provided by the municipality. On the other hand, it is common for renters to be responsible for their own trash disposal. In commercial spaces, this can be quite expensive and should be addressed in the lease. Because medical waste presents a special problem that should be addressed in the lease, you may have to make special arrangements for disposal.

INSURANCE FOR THE BUILDING AND COMMON AREAS

Customarily, the landlord will be responsible for the exterior of the building. It will be the landlord's obligation to make sure that it does not leak during rainstorms and that it is properly ventilated. Notwithstanding this fact, it is important for you to make sure the lease deals with the question of responsibility if the building is damaged and some of your records or equipment are damaged or destroyed. This responsibility signals who should purchase insurance to cover losses from damage. Insurance for common areas and exteriors of the building, even if shared by multiple tenants, could be a significant cost.

IN PLAIN ENGLISH

If you have to take out insurance for the building and its contents, including liability insurance for common areas and exterior areas, your costs will greatly increase. You should always determine who will be responsible for insuring the building before you enter into a lease.

You should find out whether it will be your obligation to obtain liability insurance for injuries that are caused in areas of the building not under your control, such as common hallways and stairwells. You should, of course, have your own liability policy for accidental injuries or accidents that occur on your leased premises. You should know going into a lease whether the landlord will pay for insurance for losses from damage and for liability to tenants and visitors for parts of the interior and exterior of the building not under your control.

SECURITY, HOURS, AND ZONING

A good lease will contain a provision dealing with security. If you are renting indoor space in a medical complex, it is likely that the landlord will be responsible for external security, although this is not universally the case. If you are renting an entire building, it is customarily your responsibility to provide whatever security you deem important. You should address the question of whether the lease permits you to install locks or alarm systems.

Your lease should also address the issue of building hours. If you have evening or weekend clinics, your lease should specify that your patients will have ready access to your office and parking facilities. If you are regularly accepting deliveries, your lease should contain a provision that will give you the flexibility you require on the time and location of deliveries. Some leases provide for heating and air conditioning to be supplied to the premises only during specific hours.

If the place you wish to rent will be used as both your personal dwelling and for business, other problems may arise. It is quite common for zoning laws to prohibit certain forms of commercial activities when the area is zoned residential. There is often an exception for health care professionals, but you should consult with your attorney before attempting to practice out of your home.

WRITTEN DOCUMENT

Finally, it is essential for you to be sure that every item agreed on between you and the landlord is stated in writing. This is particularly important when dealing with leases, since many state laws provide that a long-term lease is an interest in land and can be enforced only if in writing.

The relationship between landlords and tenants is an ancient one that is undergoing a good deal of change. Care should be taken when examining a potential location for your practice to determine exactly what you can do on the premises and whether the landlord or municipal rules will allow you to use the location for its intended purpose.

CHAPTER 9

Insurance

Recent crime statistics show that even in rural areas you may become the victim of burglary. The forces of nature—fire, floods, earthquakes—are undiscriminating in their targets. Loss of earnings through sickness or accident is a risk common to all businesses, including health care practices. And then there is the additional exposure to liability for professional negligence known more generally as *malpractice*. These risks and others are sometimes overlooked, but the potential cost makes even the slightest chance of these occurrences disastrous to a small practice. Fortunately, many of these risks can be insured against.

History contains too many gruesome stories of desperate or disturbed people obtaining insurance with an eye toward collecting the proceeds. Because of such insurance frauds, most kinds of insurance, particularly liability insurance, do not cover injuries that are intentionally caused by the policyholder.

THE BASICS OF INSURANCE LAW

Before analyzing the mechanics of choosing whether or not to insure a particular risk, a brief outline of the law of insurance is in order.

Insurable Interest

Public policy will not permit you to insure something unless you have what is called an *insurable interest*. To have an insurable interest, you must have a property right, a contract right, or a potential liability that would result in a real loss to you if a given event occurs. This rule exists in part to separate the insurance business from the gambling business—wagering on the likelihood of occurrences that you have no stake in other than your gambling stake—and to minimize the temptation to cause the calamity against which you are insured.

IN PLAIN ENGLISH

The law has gone to great lengths to try to prevent people from using insurance as a form of speculation or gambling. You must insure something in which you have a bona fide property interest, contractual interest, or exposure to liability, and that something must be at least as valuable as the amount of insurance you obtain. Many persons who have paid insurance premiums for years without ever receiving money back have fantasized about achieving a loss and getting a claim to "get their money back" from the insurer but this is illusory. Any valid insurance claim will arise from the damage to or loss of something valuable to you, so at best you only will break even on the loss and not recoup the premiums paid.

The Contract

All insurance is based on a contract between the insurer and the insured whereby the insurer assumes a specified risk for a fee called a *premium*. The insurance contract must contain at least the following:

- a definition of whatever is being insured (the subject matter);

- the nature of the risks insured against;

- the maximum possible recovery;

- the duration of the insurance; and,

- the due date and amount of the premiums.

When the amount of recovery has been predetermined in the insurance contract, it is called a *valued policy*. An *unvalued* or *open insurance policy* covers the full value of property up to a specified policy limit. There are advantages and disadvantages to each form, which will be discussed later.

The insurance industry is regulated by state law. The very documents that a company uses to make insurance contracts are regulated from state to state. Sometimes the state requires a standard form from which the company may not deviate, especially for fire insurance. A growing number of states require that plain English be used in all forms. *Plain English* is measured in reference to the average number of syllables per word and the average number of words per sentence.

After Hurricane Katrina and several other catastrophic natural events, many individuals and businesses learned, to their horror, that the insurance coverage they had was much less than they thought, and many claims for damage arising from these disasters were denied. The litigation that resulted from the insurance companies' refusals to pay claims in some cases was even more traumatic than the disasters that gave rise to the claims. The moral is clear: read your policy and be sure that you understand it. If you have any doubt, review it provision by provision with your broker and your business lawyer.

ASCERTAINING RISK

The insurance contract does more than merely shift the risk from the insured to the insurance company. The insurance industry is regulated by state law so as to spread the risk of a loss among those subject to the same risk. The risk-spreading is accomplished by defining the method used for determining the amount of the premium to be paid by the insured. First, the insurance company obtains data on the actual loss sustained by a class within a given period of time. State law regulates just how the company may define the class. An insurance company may not, for example, segregate white homeowners and nonwhite homeowners into different classes, but it may separate drivers with many accidents from drivers with few.

Next, the company divides the risk equally among the members of the class. Then the company adds a fee for administrative costs and profits. This amount is regulated from state to state. Finally, the premium is set for each individual in proportion to the likelihood that a loss will occur.

ADDITIONAL STATE REGULATION

Besides the method of determining premiums, state insurance laws usually specify the training necessary for agents and brokers, the amount of commission payable to them, and the kind of investments the insurance company may make with the premiums.

EXPECTATIONS VERSUS REALITY

One frequent result of the difficult language in which most insurance contracts are written is that the signed contract may differ in some respect from what the agent may have led the insured to expect. If you can prove that an agent actually misled you, the agent will be personally liable to you for the amount of promised coverage. In addition, the insurance company itself may be liable for the wrongful acts of its agent.

Most often, the agent will not lie, but will unintentionally neglect to inform the insured of some detail. For instance, if you want insurance for transporting expensive equipment, the agent may sell you a policy that covers transport only in public carriers when you intended to rent a truck and transport the equipment yourself. In most states, the courts hold that it is the duty of the insured (you) to read the policy before signing. If, in the preceding example, you neglected to read the clause that limits coverage to a public carrier, you would be out of luck. Failure to read the policy is not considered a valid excuse.

In other states, this doctrine has been considered too harsh. These states will allow an insured to challenge specific provisions in the contract to the extent that they do not conform to reasonable expectations resulting from promises that the agent made. In the preceding example, it might be considered reasonable to expect that you would be insured when transporting your own goods. If the agent did not specifically call your attention to this limitation in the contract, odds are that you would have a good case for getting rid of it. In addition, it is common for the insured to receive the policy only after the premium is paid or only after a specific request to see the policy is made.

Other states follow a different approach for contract interpretation and attempt to ascertain the intention of the parties. The first step in interpreting an insurance policy is to examine the actual terms of the contract, as they are supposed to reflect what the parties agreed to. It is important to read the text with a view to the context of the policy as a whole—what was the insured trying to achieve by purchasing the insurance, and was that purpose communicated to the agent who produced the policy in response to that request? If, after the examination of the text and the context, two or more conflicting interpretations remain and are reasonable, the ambiguity will be resolved against the insurer. A court in these states will assume that parties to an insurance contract do not create meaningless provisions and will favor the interpretation that lets all provisions have meaning.

IN PLAIN ENGLISH

Even in the most liberal, insured-friendly state, it is not advisable simply to wait for the agent to point out defects or potentially unexpected variations in the contract. You should read the contract with the agent. If it is unintelligible, ask the agent to list on a separate sheet all the important aspects before you sign, and then keep that sheet with the contract.

OVERINSURING AND UNDERINSURING

If an insured accidentally overvalues his or her property, the insurance coverage still will apply. The recovery, however, will only be for the actual value of the property. Overinsurance does not entitle you to recover more than the actual value of the property insured even though it usually means you paid a higher premium for your insurance coverage. (Remember what we said about insurance not being a form of speculation for profit—one does not have an insurable interest beyond the actual value of the property.)

Since you can, at best, break even with insurance, you might think it would be profitable to underinsure your property. You could gain by paying lower premiums and lose only in the event that the damage exceeds the policy maximum. This has been tried but without success.

> **EXAMPLE:** An insured stated the value of her unscheduled property as $9,950 and obtained insurance on that amount. (*Unscheduled property* means an undetermined collection of goods—for example, all of a doctor's waiting room furniture and office equipment—that may change from time to time.) A fire occurred, causing at least $9,950 in damage.
>
> The insurance company investigated the claim and determined that the insured owned at least $36,500 in unscheduled property. The company refused to pay on the grounds that the insured obtained the insurance fraudulently. The court agreed with the insurance company, stating that the intentional failure to communicate the full value of the unscheduled property rendered the entire contract void. Therefore, the insured could not even collect the policy maximum.

Although at first glance this outcome may seem harsh, its ultimate fairness becomes apparent with a little analysis. The chance of losing $9,950 out of $36,500 is greater than the chance of losing $9,950 out of $9,950, simply because most accidents or thefts do not result in total losses. In this case, the insured should not have paid premiums for $9,950 coverage because she belonged in a much higher risk category.

Various tests are used by the courts to determine whether an omission or misstatement renders a policy void. In almost every case, the omission or misstatement must be intentional or obviously reckless, and it must be material to the contract. Materiality typically is measured with reference to the degree of importance that the insurance company ascribes to the omitted or misstated fact. If stating the fact correctly would have significantly affected the conditions or premiums that the company would demand, the fact is likely to be material. In the previous example, had the full value of the unscheduled property been stated, the insurer would either have demanded that the full value be insured or that a higher premium be paid for the limited coverage. Thus, the misstatement clearly was material.

UNINTENTIONAL UNDERVALUING

Not all undervaluations will be material, and many insurance contracts allow some undervaluation where it is unintentional. This provision is designed to protect the insured from inflation, which causes property to increase in replacement value before the policy's renewal date.

A so-called *coinsurance clause* generally provides that the insured may recover 100% of any loss up to the face value of the policy, provided the property is insured for at least 80% of its full value. Check your policy to see if it includes such a clause and, if so, what percentage of the value must be insured.

> **EXAMPLE:** If a building worth $100,000 was insured for $80,000 and suffered a $79,000 loss from a covered casualty, the insured would recover the full amount of the loss, or $79,000. If the property was insured for only $50,000, on the other hand, the following formula would be used to

determine the amount of recovery: divide the amount of insurance coverage ($50,000) by the total value of the property ($100,000) and multiply the resulting fraction (½) by the loss ($79,000) to get the recovery ($39,500).

IN PLAIN ENGLISH

It is important to carry insurance on at least 80% of the value of your property. Considering inflation, it is wise to reexamine your coverage each year. Some policies automatically increase the coverage annually based on a fixed percentage.

PROPERTY COVERED

All insurance policies are limited to certain defined subject matter and to losses caused to that subject matter by certain defined risks. Once the risks are recognized, it is a simple matter to decide whether to insure against them. Correctly defining the subject matter of insurance, however, is tricky business. Mistakes here are not uncommon and can result in any one of us finding ourselves uninsured.

Scheduling Property

The typical insurance policy will contain various exclusions and exemptions. For example, most homeowner and auto insurance policies cover personal property but exclude business property. If you keep certain items, such as your library of books on the history of Chinese medicine, at home, are the books personal or business property? The answer depends on whether you ever use the books in your practice. If you do, this may convert them to business property, even though you keep them at home.

In order to avoid the potentially uninsured loss of such property, you may *schedule* the pieces that are held for business use. *Scheduling* is a form of inventorying where the insured submits a list and description of all pieces to be insured with an appraisal of their value. The insurer assumes the risk of all scheduled items without concern as to whether they pertain to the business or not. Insurance on scheduled property is slightly more expensive than that of unscheduled property.

Valuing Scheduled Property

Many battles occur over the value of objects stolen, destroyed, or lost. In anticipation of such battles, you should maintain records and receipts to establish the market price of your property and an inventory of all property on hand. In the case of certain kinds of property (artwork or antiques, for example), the value must be determined by an expert in the field. However, this will not avoid all problems because the insurance company can always contest the scheduled value.

WHAT AND WHEN TO INSURE

When you are uncertain as to whether something should be insured, there are several factors to consider in making your decision. First, you must set a value on that which is to be insured. Life and health are of the utmost value and should be insured. Material goods are valued according to the cost of replacement. If you keep a large inventory of goods or if you own expensive equipment, it probably should be insured. The most elementary way to determine whether the value is sufficiently high to necessitate insurance is to rely on the pain factor: if it would hurt to lose it, insure it.

Second, you must estimate the chances that a given calamity will occur. An insurance broker can tell you what risks are prevalent in your particular type of practice. You should supplement this information with your personal knowledge. For example, you may know that your office is virtually fireproof or that only a massive flood would cause any real damage. Although these facts should be weighed in your decision, you should not be guilty of audaciously tempting fate, for, as the great tragedians have recounted, to scoff at disaster is to invite it. And if the odds are truly slim but some risk is still present, the premium likely will be correspondingly smaller.

Finally, the cost of the insurance should be considered. Bear in mind that insurance purchased to cover your business is tax-deductible.

KEEPING INSURANCE COSTS DOWN

As previously discussed, the premiums charged by insurance companies are, to some extent, determined by law. Nonetheless, it still pays to shop around. Insurance companies compete by offering a variety of different packages.

COMMON INSURABLE RISKS

There are certain risks that are common to the health care industry and thus deserve special mention. These risks fall into roughly four categories: protection of your building and its contents (*property insurance*), protection against malpractice (*professional liability insurance*), protection of the health of you and your employees (*health insurance*), and *disability insurance*.

IN PLAIN ENGLISH

In your practice, you should consider insuring against losses relating to:

- property, both the physical building and its contents;

- liability for injuries to patients, visitors, and others caused by you or your employees;

- professional liability (malpractice) for injuries to patients;

- health insurance for you and your employees; and,

- disability insurance for you and your employees.

Property Insurance

The choice of insurance with respect to your building and its contents will depend on whether you own the building or are a tenant. If you are an owner, you will need to obtain insurance on your building to protect against loss from fire and possibly vandalism; if you are a tenant, you will need to check your lease to see if you are responsible for purchasing this insurance. If you are in an area that is prone to earthquakes, flooding, tornadoes, or hurricanes, you probably can get an extended coverage endorsement (usually attached to your fire insurance policy) to cover loss under these particular circumstances. Be sure that you understand the losses covered and not covered regarding water damage—many victims of Hurricane Katrina wish that they had. If you are leasing space, in most cases you need only consider insuring the contents of your premises, but be sure that your lease does not impose some risks on you relating to the building, its exterior areas, or its common areas that you might be forced to insure.

Insurance on building contents is a separate contract, although it is usually combined with the policy on the building itself. You will want to consider obtaining fire and theft insurance on most, if not all, of your lab and office equipment, files, inventory, and so forth.

A common form of insurance obtained by professionals is *general liability* insurance. This insurance may be combined with personal and real property insurance and may include *premises liability coverage*—protection against "slip-and-fall" type injuries; *non-owned automobile coverage*—protection against liability for auto accidents that occur during work hours but in a privately owned car (for example, if an employee uses his or her car to deliver X-rays to a hospital and gets in an accident while on the way back to your office); and *employee negligence coverage*—protection against negligent acts committed by your employees (this is not professional liability insurance). A policy that covers all of these risks often is referred to as a *comprehensive general liability policy*, but as with all insurance, consult your insurance agent or attorney to make sure the policy you are considering truly covers all the risks that you want it to cover.

Business interruption insurance, often purchased in connection with a property insurance policy, covers lost income resulting from property damage or loss. For example, if your building is seriously damaged by a fire and it is three months before the building is restored, business interruption insurance would cover the profits you would have earned during that period, as well as operating expenses incurred despite the building's unusability.

Professional Liability Insurance

It is no secret that malpractice claims have become one of the occupational hazards of the health care industry. The medical profession has probably seen the greatest increase in malpractice claims of all the professions. Although medical professionals are the most susceptible to malpractice claims, all health care professionals are exposed to potential liability. One successful claim can wipe you out if you are not properly insured. Consequently, professional liability insurance should be considered a necessity.

Professional liability insurance is quite complex. Due to the extreme importance of maintaining sufficient coverage, it is highly advised that you consult with a local attorney who is knowledgeable in the field of malpractice and insurance defense. There are two important issues you need to be familiar with before consulting an attorney and obtaining coverage.

Coverage

Malpractice results when an injury is sustained due to a practitioner's substandard care. Professional liability insurance covers claims arising only from such substandard care. It will not cover intentionally injurious or criminal acts. It usually will not cover acts of sexual misconduct (although a rider may). It usually does not cover claims arising from injuries sustained from improperly maintained premises (office, waiting room, and parking lot, for example)—although a general liability policy (discussed earlier) should.

A professional liability policy may cover negligent acts committed by your employees within the scope of their employment. Since you may be liable for such acts, it is important that you check your policy to see whether you are covered, or whether your employees should be identified as "additional insureds" under the policy.

Policies vary with respect to the costs that are covered. Some policies cover only the actual damages awarded to the successful *claimant* (patient). Other policies also cover the cost of defending against the malpractice claim. The difference can be critical. For example, assume that a practitioner has $5,000,000 worth of coverage that covers only damages actually awarded. The patient successfully brings a malpractice suit and recovers $700,000 in damages. The attorney's fees for defending the practitioner total $120,000. Even though the practitioner is covered well in excess of the damages awarded and attorney's fees, the practitioner is personally liable for the $120,000 owed to the attorney. Defending malpractice suits is generally very expensive, so check to make sure that your policy covers the costs of litigation. Policies that do not include attorney's fees are extremely rare.

Practitioners frequently ask, "How much coverage do I need?" There is no formula that dictates how much insurance is enough, although a common answer is, "Enough to allow you to sleep at night." It is important to remember that the best insurance is to maintain a proper standard of care—you could easily go broke trying to keep "enough" insurance coverage. A hospital, clinic, or practice plan may specify certain coverage amounts that must be carried.

There are certain coverage limits to be aware of. Coverage may be limited to the policy's effective period, or it may be limited on a per-person basis. To illustrate, assume the policy is for $5,000,000 worth of coverage for one year. If it is limited on a period basis, the policy will cover any claim(s) made during that year, up to an aggregate of $5,000,000. If it is limited on a per-person basis, on the other hand, the policy will cover $5,000,000 worth of claims per person made during that year. Such a policy will have a cap—say, up to $15,000,000—so that a thoroughly incompetent practitioner does not bankrupt the insurer.

Types of Policies

There are two types of professional liability policies—*occurrence* and *claims-made*. Occurrence policies have become less common in recent years. Due to the nature of their coverage, carriers have been less inclined to write such policies.

An *occurrence policy* covers claims that occur during the period of coverage. For example, say that a practitioner is covered from January 1, 2009, through December 31, 2009, (one year, for simplicity's sake) and he or she negligently delivers a child on June 1, 2009. Regardless of when a claim is finally made, the practitioner is covered. Complications may not develop for many years, yet the policy will retroactively cover the claim since the event occurred during the period of coverage. This possibility of delayed liability is precisely why many carriers refuse to write such policies. Those who do write them generally charge a proportionately higher premium than for a comparable amount of claims-made coverage.

Claims-made policies are limited to claims that are actually made during the period of coverage. Assume the same facts as in the previous example. Complications, as a result of the improper delivery, do not develop until January 1, 2010, at which time a malpractice claim is filed. Since the practitioner was covered by a claims-made policy only during 2009, the claim is not covered, even though the act of malpractice occurred during the period of coverage. Since it is common for complications to develop years after an act of malpractice has occurred, it is important that there not be any gaps in your claims-made coverage.

Gaps in insurance coverage may occur when you take an extended sabbatical or retire from the profession altogether. If you have been covered during your entire practice by an occurrence policy, there is no cause for concern regarding potential gaps in your policy. There are two scenarios where gaps in coverage commonly occur.

First, if you are converting a claims-made policy into an occurrence policy at the end of the earlier policy's life, you will need to obtain *nose coverage* attached to the occurrence policy, as well as the occurrence policy itself, to cover a gap that now exists. Nose coverage protects against acts of malpractice that have occurred prior to the beginning of the occurrence policy but for which no claim is made until after the claims-made policy has ended. As an alternative, you could purchase *tail coverage* for the claims-made policy, which, in essence, extends the coverage for that policy.

Second, a gap in coverage will occur where you have been covered by a claims-made policy up to a particular point in time, at which time you no longer need coverage (for example, you are retiring, changing insurers, or stepping down your practice to a lower-risk specialty), so the policy is terminated. If an act of malpractice occurred during your practice, but a claim is made after you have retired, you will not be covered unless you obtain tail coverage. *Tail coverage* protects against claims that arise after an earlier policy has lapsed or been terminated. Both nose and tail coverage can be expensive—from one-and-one-half to two times your annual premium—but are necessary to prevent gaps in coverage from occurring. Many policies provide some tail coverage free of charge if you have been insured for an extended period of time. It is a good idea to review your professional liability coverage each year. Waiting to find out that your coverage is inadequate until a claim is made would be disastrous.

Health Insurance

Employers often provide health benefits (medical, dental, and vision coverage) to their employees as an employment benefit. If you choose to provide this benefit, it is unwise for you to render health care to your employees in lieu of purchasing insurance. In the unlikely event of unsatisfactory treatment, the relationship between you and your employee would be jeopardized. Therefore, it is more prudent to obtain insurance coverage for your employees' health, dental, and vision needs and insist that they seek treatment from another practitioner. With the ever-increasing prevalence of managed care organizations, many employers have turned to policies written by one of the popular *health maintenance organizations* (HMOs) or *preferred provider organizations* (PPOs) for their employee health care needs. Group insurance plans, whether sponsored by a health care network or by a collective of professionals, most likely will allow you to purchase the insurance at a lower rate.

Disability Insurance

The importance of including disability insurance as a part of your benefit program cannot be overemphasized, considering that in the event of disability, the professional's financial needs remain constant or may even increase, while earnings potential is curtailed.

While it is theoretically possible for the individual to establish a savings program so that funds will be available in the event of a disabling occurrence, in reality such a self-funded program is impractical for many reasons, including the fact that implementation of a savings program takes time, which could be interrupted by a disability or by other requirements for those funds.

Accordingly, the most practical method of accommodating this need is through the acquisition of a disability insurance policy. There are two general types. The first provides benefits through a group contract. This is similar in many respects to group-term life insurance. The second category provides benefits through policies issued directly to individuals. These may be funded directly by individual employees or by the employer.

There are tax considerations that might influence your selection of a particular type of program, and you are well-advised to consult with your tax adviser and a financial planner with expertise in employee benefit programs before making your selection. The contracts themselves contain numerous complex terms and involve careful planning. For instance, some policies cover you if you cannot work in your chosen profession while others cover you only if you cannot work at all. Your professional advisers should be able to evaluate the various policies and their terms and recommend the one that best fits your situation.

CHAPTER 10

Malpractice

The term *malpractice* has been overused to describe many different forms of misconduct. Ethical violations, fraud, breach of fiduciary duty, battery, and invasion of privacy are the most common forms of misconduct that are frequently referred to as malpractice. But malpractice is really just a specialized form of negligence, called *professional negligence*.

IN PLAIN ENGLISH

Professional negligence is a form of negligence, which is a failure to use ordinary and reasonable care that breaches a duty owed to a person and causes an injury to that person. Because professionals are required to have special training and expertise, they are held to a higher standard of care. Professionals must use the degree of skill, care, and diligence exercised by members of the same profession practicing in similar circumstances.

There are numerous texts and multivolume treatises you can consult for an in-depth discussion of malpractice in the health care professions. Our discussion in this chapter, intended only to give a general overview to aid in making decisions that will reduce exposure to liability, covers:

- the factors courts consider in determining whether a practitioner has committed malpractice;

- the defenses that are available once a claim has been made; and,

- your liability for the wrongful acts of others.

NEGLIGENCE IN GENERAL

Negligence is a term used to describe a basis for liability that results from a failure to perform a duty that the law requires under a given set of circumstances. Generally, the duty that the law imposes is a duty to use *due care*, or to "exercise the prudence that a reasonable person would exercise in similar circumstances."

> **EXAMPLE:** It is considered negligent for a person who has extremely poor vision to attempt to drive without glasses, based on the theory that a reasonable person would not attempt to drive under the circumstances.

Professional negligence is simply an extension of the negligence theory to circumstances where an individual is held to a higher standard of care as a result of special skills or knowledge that he or she holds him- or herself out as possessing. In order for a patient to prevail on a claim of professional negligence, he or she must prove that there was some duty flowing from the health care provider to the patient, that the duty was breached, and that the patient was injured as a result.

The duty that flows from the health care professional to the patient arises as a consequence of the relationship between the two parties. By accepting responsibility for treatment, the practitioner implies that he or she will use the proper care and diligence in the exercise of the advanced skills and knowledge he or she possesses to accomplish the purpose for which employed. The law also imposes this duty on the practitioner.

The duty owed to the patient is the practitioner's conforming to a certain accepted standard of care. The practitioner's conduct is judged against this standard to determine whether or not he or she is liable for professional negligence.

THE STANDARD OF CARE

All persons are held to certain minimum standards in the activities they undertake. If, however, a person acquires special competence, he or she is held to a standard commensurate with his or her superior knowledge and skills. Consequently, because health care professionals possess knowledge, skills, and training superior to that of the ordinary person, the law imposes a higher standard of care upon them.

The standard of care to which health care professionals are held is measured by "the degree of knowledge, skill, and care ordinarily possessed and employed by members of the profession in good standing." Obviously, the kind of conduct required will vary among the different health care professions, depending on the standard of care customarily exercised by members of that branch of the profession. In addition, if the practitioner holds him- or herself out as a specialist in a particular field, he or she will be required to act as a reasonably competent specialist in the same or similar circumstances.

Regardless of the particular field of health care, the practitioner is not required to be endowed with extraordinary knowledge and skill, though he or she is required to keep abreast of the times and to practice in accordance with recognized methods of treatment.

Whether or not a practitioner has deviated from the accepted standard of care is largely dependent upon the particular facts of each case. The law recognizes that many times, under a given set of facts, there may be more than one acceptable method of treatment that meets the standard of care. Consequently, the practitioner is not judged in hindsight; that is, liability cannot be based on the fact that it later appears that another approach would have been more successful. Furthermore, the practitioner is entitled to have the propriety of his or her conduct judged according to the practices of the particular school of medicine to which the practitioner belongs. Courts have held that the school must be recognized and that a respectable minority of practitioners must follow the principles in order for the school to be legitimate. However, the practitioner still must properly administer the particular school's techniques; the practitioner cannot conceal his or her incompetence behind a veil of professional opinion.

In a dwindling minority of states, courts also give consideration to the particular type of community in which the practitioner practices when determining whether the standard of care has been met. In other words, if the practitioner practices in a remote rural area, where equipment and facilities are inferior to those of more urban areas, the practitioner's conduct will be judged according to the standard of practitioners in that (or a similar) rural community, not against other practitioners in general. This rule has fallen into disfavor over the years as technological advances in communication and transportation have made access possible to even the most remote areas. In addition, many practitioners are now board-certified in accordance with national standards.

BREACH OF DUTY

The practitioner is required to carefully and completely utilize his or her knowledge and skill in an attempt to diagnose and treat the patient's ailment. An honest error in judgment, made in the course of following a procedure or administering a treatment, that is recognized as acceptable within the particular school of medicine does not create liability.

Liability arises only when the practitioner breaches the standard of care. A breach of the standard occurs where the practitioner deviates from the recognized standards of care. Examples of conduct that would breach the requisite standard of care include performance of an unauthorized operation not justified by a medical emergency, commission of a technical error during a surgical procedure, failure to obtain a proper medical history, failure to refer a specialist when one is necessary, failure to carefully conduct a thorough physical examination, and failure to timely diagnose a condition.

Of course, if no damage results from the practitioner's deviation from the standard of care, there can be no liability. Likewise, the patient must prove that the particular breach of duty was the substantial contributing cause of the injury.

Whether or not a particular act or omission is the substantial contributing cause of an injury is often a very complex issue to resolve. Essentially, the decision is arrived at by use of expert testimony.

> **EXAMPLE:** A physician prescribes a drug without determining whether the patient will have any adverse reactions. The patient later operates an automobile and blacks out while at the wheel because of a reaction to the drug that the doctor should have predicted if she had carefully examined the patient's history. The patient's car runs into a power pole, causing a blackout in a nearby city, where a person falls down the stairs in the dark and breaks his leg. The practitioner would certainly be liable for any injury to the patient, but is the practitioner also liable to the individual who broke his leg? Granted, the facts in this scenario are somewhat farfetched, but the example serves to illustrate the complexities that the causation issue raises.

Only where an aggrieved patient has proven all the necessary factors can he or she recover monetary damages from the practitioner. In addition to civil liability to the patient, a practitioner guilty of malpractice may also face license suspension or revocation.

INFORMED CONSENT

An increasing number of malpractice cases have involved the doctrine of *informed consent*. Health care professionals are required to provide their patients with sufficient information to permit the patient to make well-informed decisions regarding their treatment. Treatment without full disclosure of material risks and viable alternatives involved is another form of professional negligence.

Generally, a claim will arise where the patient consents based on insufficient information and later suffers damage as a result. The patient then brings suit, alleging that consent would not have been given had he or she been better informed of the risks involved. The procedure may have been perfectly performed, yet due to the fact that the patient was not fully informed of the material risks and viable alternatives involved, the practitioner may be liable for any adverse consequences that are normally considered an acceptable risk or side effect of the procedure.

Under the doctrine of informed consent, the health care provider has a duty to explain the nature of the procedure and to inform the patient of the material risks involved with the proposed treatment, as well as the possible alternative forms of treatment that may be available. An injured patient must prove that the practitioner failed to provide an explanation of the procedure, the material risks, or the viable alternatives. In addition, the patient must prove that he or she would not have undergone treatment had he or she known the risk of the harm that, in fact, occurred.

The duty to inform is not absolute under all circumstances; there are some limitations. The most significant limitation is that the risk at issue must be *material* (or significant enough) to trigger the duty to inform. Most courts today test materiality in terms of whether a reasonable person in the patient's position would be likely to attach significance to the risk in deciding whether or not to undergo the proposed treatment (the so-called *objective test*); a minority of states still test materiality from the individual's perspective—whether this patient would have consented to this procedure had he or she been fully informed (the *subjective test*). Whether the patient will attach significance to the risk is determined by weighing the likelihood of a particular injury occurring, along with the seriousness of that injury. If the risk of serious injury is high, the practitioner will be compelled to disclose the information.

Unfortunately, the tests courts use to determine whether a risk is material do not provide a clear answer to the question of whether to disclose the risk. Consequently, the safest decision is to always provide the patient with complete information regarding:

- the actual procedure involved in the treatment to be undertaken;

- the risks associated with that treatment; and,

- any alternative forms of treatment and the risks posed by those treatments.

It is best to have the patient sign a written form containing the information, although if that is problematic, you may choose to document your conversation in the medical chart or use other means to establish that the necessary information was provided to the patient in order to obtain the informed consent.

Other limitations on the informed consent doctrine include what is known as a *therapeutic privilege* to withhold information, where disclosure of the risk would be detrimental to the well-being of the patient. For example, a surgeon may not want to disclose to his suicidal patient that the operation about to be performed will most likely result in sterilization. This becomes a matter of professional judgment. However, the practitioner should tell a relative (or legal guardian) of the probable risks involved. Again, you are well-advised to document such withholding of information, the reasons for doing so, and the names of the relatives or guardians you notified.

The practitioner is not required to disclose risks where an emergency situation precludes the practitioner from making disclosure (for example, where the patient needs immediate attention and he or she is unconscious, or is a minor or incompetent and the parent or guardian is not present). Nor is the practitioner required to disclose risks that are immaterial, obvious, remote, or already known to the patient.

It should be noted that in many states, a practitioner will be liable for *battery* where treatment is completely unauthorized yet performed anyway. For example, a physician who removed a patient's tonsils without consent during surgery on the patient's nose was found liable for battery. This situation differs from the informed consent cases since the treatment is administered without any form of consent from the patient.

DEFENSES

Health care professionals are not required to be the guarantors of all diagnoses and cures. As was indicated earlier, some latitude is afforded for honest mistakes in judgment. In addition, there are several defenses to a claim of professional negligence.

Good Samaritan Defense

Most states have what are known as *Good Samaritan statutes*. These statutes were enacted to encourage persons to give aid to others in emergency situations, and therefore, in the majority of states, are applicable to nonmedical persons as well. The statutes vary from state to state, but they attempt to limit, in some way, the liability of a Good Samaritan under emergency circumstances.

The Good Samaritan defense is generally not available away from the scene of the emergency. In addition, in most states the person giving aid must be acting in good faith. This requirement generally has been interpreted to mean that the person giving aid must not be guilty of gross negligence.

Contributory Negligence or Comparative Negligence

Contributory or comparative negligence is an additional defense. *Contributory negligence* is conduct by the patient that contributes to the cause of or aggravates his or her own injuries. For example, assume that a patient sees an orthopedic specialist, complaining of pain in his shoulder. The specialist negligently fails to diagnose a fracture but advises the patient to see his family physician. The patient fails to see his family physician and later suffers complications from the fracture. If the patient later sues the bone specialist for negligence, the specialist can raise contributory negligence as a defense because the patient acted negligently, too, in failing to follow the advice that was given to him, and in doing so aggravated his injuries.

IN PLAIN ENGLISH

Patients still have a duty to exercise reasonable and ordinary care for themselves before and after they are injured, and a breach of that duty can be deemed to be negligence. If a patient acts negligently and aggravates or contributes to his or her own injuries, the law will reduce his or her recovery for those injuries. This form of negligence is referred to as *contributory negligence* in those jurisdictions that use it as a bar to all recovery, or *comparative negligence* in those states where the patient's negligence is compared to the doctor's professional negligence and the patient's recovery, if any, is reduced by the percentage of fault for the injuries that is attributed to the patient's own negligent actions.

In a few states, contributory negligence is a complete bar to any recovery by the patient. Consequently, in the previous example, the patient would be denied any monetary recovery if a jury were to determine that he was contributorily negligent.

In other states, the defense is known as *comparative negligence*, which falls into two categories. The first, known as *pure comparative negligence*, permits the plaintiff to recover, regardless of his or her fault, so long as the defendant is responsible for at least 1% of the fault. Under *modified comparative negligence*, the plaintiff may not recover at all if he or she is equally or more at fault than the defendant. The percentage of fault attributable to the plaintiff reduces the amount of the recovery by that same percentage instead of absolutely denying the plaintiff recovery. Under the pure comparative fault standard, if a jury found that the patient was 60% responsible for his injuries, they would reduce the patient's award by 60%. Under the modified form of comparative fault, the patient would recover nothing because his fault was greater than 50%.

Statutes of Limitations

Finally, all states have *statutes of limitation*, which put a time limit on when a lawsuit for malpractice may be brought. These statutes vary among states. Some states have engaged in tort reform that has shortened the statutes of limitation for malpractice, thus allowing claims to be time-barred earlier. In addition, the rules vary as to when the statute *tolls* (is suspended) and begins to run. Consequently, it is advisable to consult with your attorney on this and other matters that relate to professional liability.

VICARIOUS LIABILITY

Vicarious liability, or liability for the mistakes of others, is an issue that occasionally arises in the area of professional malpractice. In a private practice setting where two or more practitioners treat the same patient, neither is liable for the negligence of the other unless there is a *concert of action* between the practitioners—that is, they purposefully acted together in the action or occurrence.

> **EXAMPLE:** Where a dentist determines that a patient needs his wisdom teeth removed and refers the patient to an oral surgeon for the procedure, the dentist will not be liable for any negligent acts committed by the oral surgeon. Had the dentist and the surgeon acted jointly, each would be liable regardless of the fact that one or the other had a more active role in the procedure.

Normally, a hospital staff physician is not liable for the negligence of hospital employees; however, under certain circumstances the physician will be liable. This occurs when the hospital employee is acting under the direct supervision of the physician, such as a scrub nurse in the operating room. In this case, both the employer hospital and the physician can be held liable.

Unfortunately, the law provides little guidance in determining when action is or is not joint action. Incorporating the practice or using another limited liability device (discussed in Chapter 1) can reduce the problem of vicarious liability in the majority of states.

The majority of health care professionals will adhere to the high standards of their respected professions and do everything in their power to avoid acts that might be considered malpractice. Unfortunately, unexpected problems occasionally arise. One of the best ways to avoid liability is to be aware of the current state of the law on the subject and maintain complete and legible patient records. As with most areas of law, when you perceive the possibility of a problem, it is essential to immediately seek professional assistance from an attorney who specializes in the field of medical malpractice defense. Customarily, the attorney will be provided by your malpractice insurance carrier, or you might want to contact your professional association for some recommendations.

CHAPTER 11

Licensing and Hospital Privileges

Health care professionals, like most other professionals, must acquire and maintain licenses to practice their professions. The license serves as a symbol of that person's qualification to practice in a particular field of health care. The license is not a right; that is, successful completion of the required education and training does not entitle the practitioner to a license. A professional license is a privilege, and like any other privilege, it can be suspended, revoked, or denied for any of several reasons.

This chapter is not intended to teach you all you need to know about qualifying for a license to practice your health care profession in the United States—we are sure that you are intimately familiar with those requirements if you are pursuing or have obtained a license to practice. Instead, in this chapter, we will provide a broad overview of the licensing process from a legal perspective. We will discuss licensing requirements and reasons for license denial, suspension, or revocation. In addition, we will discuss from a legal perspective the relationship between practitioners and hospitals, commonly referred to as *staff privileges*.

A PRIVILEGE, NOT A RIGHT

As previously noted, a license to practice medicine, dentistry, chiropractic, and other healing professions is bestowed as a matter of privilege. It is not a contract with the state. It merely signifies that the practitioner has complied with the procedural requirements and possesses the necessary qualifications to be granted the privilege to practice in that particular state. Once the license has been obtained, the practitioner does not then gain an unrestricted right to practice. The state still has the power to restrain or regulate the practitioner during the course of his or her practice.

Each state has its own licensing requirements. Usually, a Board of Examiners or some other administrative agency oversees the licensing process. Generally, each discipline of the healing arts has a corresponding examining board, for example, the Board of Dentistry. Some states have boards that oversee more than one discipline. For example, Oregon's Board of Medical Examiners oversees the licensing of physicians (MDs and DOs), podiatrists, acupuncturists, and physician's assistants. Each state's statutes prescribe which of the healing arts require licensing. Most states require a license to practice as a physician, surgeon, dentist, nurse, chiropractor, or optometrist. In addition, many statutes provide exemptions from the licensing requirements. For example, in many states the licensing statutes of state A do not apply to a practitioner who is licensed in state B but is in state A for purposes of consultation with another practitioner who is licensed in state A.

LICENSING REQUIREMENTS

Since licensing is regulated at the state level, the requirements will vary from state to state. It would be impractical to discuss each state's various requirements in this book. You are advised to check with your own state licensing board for the specific, detailed requirements of your state.

Although state licensing statutes do not generally say that only natural persons may acquire a license, most states have held this by implication; therefore, corporations generally are not allowed to acquire a license to practice a healing art—only humans may obtain a license.

Most, if not all, statutes require that the applicant possess the intellectual fitness and qualification to practice a particular branch of health care. Generally, this is evidenced by completion of a professional education. In many states, a diploma from a qualifying institution serves as evidence of the fitness and qualification of the applicant to practice. Some states have more specific requirements that dictate that certain courses must be satisfactorily completed or a certain number of hours of education are necessary to establish fitness and qualification. Most states require proof of moral fitness as well. The applicant must be of solid character—trustworthy, reliable, and honest. Acts of *moral turpitude* (fraud or theft, for example) committed in the past may disqualify the applicant from acquiring a license.

IN PLAIN ENGLISH

Requirements for the licensing of health care professionals vary from state to state, but in general you must demonstrate the following.

- *Intellectual fitness.* This is generally established by passing required professional education courses or obtaining a degree; often, too, you must pass the "Boards"—an exam sponsored by the state Board of Examiners.

- *Moral fitness.* You must show that you are trustworthy, reliable, and honest.

Many states require the satisfactory completion of an examination given by the appropriate Board of Examiners. Some states also require proof that the applicant has obtained professional liability (malpractice) insurance as a prerequisite to licensing.

Most, if not all, states require the payment of a fee to obtain the license. The fee is administrative and covers the cost of the investigation of the applicant, examination fees, and the general review of the application. Finally, most states have reciprocity provisions, which may enable licensed practitioners from other states to practice in the licensing state without the necessity of complying with all the first-time applicant procedures.

Once the Board of Examiners has all the relevant documentation and information, it makes a decision whether to grant the applicant a license. If the license is denied, a satisfactory explanation must be given to the applicant. The applicant may or may not then have an opportunity to be heard at a hearing. State licensing boards are subject to the prohibitions of the United States Constitution. Consequently, licensing decisions may not be based upon impermissible or discriminatory reasons such as an applicant's race or sex.

DENIAL, SUSPENSION, OR REVOCATION OF A LICENSE TO PRACTICE

The denial, suspension, or revocation of a license must be based on the premise that the applicant or practitioner is or has become unfit to practice. Since the license is a privilege, denial or revocation for good cause universally is accepted as legal. However, the actions of the board must afford you appropriate due process, which generally means that you must be given enough information to understand the reason for the determination and some opportunity to challenge it.

Denial

A license may be denied for various reasons. If the applicant fails to meet any of the qualifying requirements or criteria, the license can be denied. The licensing board may not deny a license based on discriminatory reasons. Obviously, if a denial were based partially on the fact that the applicant was a member of a minority race, the denial would be a violation of the applicant's constitutional rights.

Suspension and Revocation

In order for a licensing board to suspend or revoke a license, there must be a showing of *good cause*, or sufficient grounds. Each state has the power to define by statute which forms of conduct, if engaged in, will result in license suspension or revocation (as well as criminal liability in some instances). Some states have held that revocation may be based only on the acts proscribed by statute. That is, a practitioner cannot have his or her license revoked for a reason not specifically set forth within the statute.

As the qualification requirements vary between the states, so do the grounds for revocation. Immoral or unprofessional conduct is a common ground for revocation in most, if not all, states. It is also the most difficult to establish. Most courts and licensing boards have construed these statutes to mean that a minor breach of professional ethics or act of unprofessional conduct does not justify license revocation.

Conduct that has been held to be unprofessional and resulted in license revocation includes:

- the fraudulent representation that the patient has a disease or ailment in order to extort a fee;

- the fraudulent representation that the practitioner can cure an incurable disease to extract a fee;

- immoral acts committed against patients (such as having a sexual relationship with a patient);

- false or misleading advertising (actual fraud and attempts to deceive generally are grounds for revocation; simply failing to follow the local advertising rules of a professional association is not generally grounds for revocation); and,

■ repeated acts of incompetence (generally, an isolated incident is not grounds for revocation unless it was a gross error).

When the quality of treatment administered to a particular patient is called into question, the licensing board (or in some states, the disciplinary board) may hold a hearing or contested case proceeding. The practitioner's course of treatment with respect to that patient is scrutinized, and, if it is determined that the practitioner engaged in negligent conduct, the board can impose punishment ranging from probation to license revocation (depending on the severity of the error). Most statutes provide for revocation of a license that was initially procured through fraud or misrepresentation, for example, where a practitioner misrepresents that he has never engaged in or been arrested for acts of moral turpitude, when in fact he has.

IN PLAIN ENGLISH

Moral turpitude is an act that reveals a lack of trustworthiness or faithfulness. It includes acts that reveal an immoral mind-set, such as lying, cheating, or committing a criminal act involving deception or immorality. Patients are in a relationship of trust with their physicians, and are expected to enjoy faithful and honest treatment from health care professionals. Acts that breach this trust are evidence of moral turpitude.

Revocation is required in many states where the practitioner allows or aids an unlicensed person to practice. For example, where practitioner A employs practitioner B and B is not licensed to practice in A's state, A would be guilty of aiding the unlicensed practice of health care and B would be guilty of practicing without a license.

Practicing under an assumed or false name is grounds for revocation in most, if not all, states. Likewise, the false designation of title—that is, the practitioner's claim that he or she is licensed to practice a particular specialty, when in fact he or she is not—is almost universally grounds for revocation.

Where a practitioner has engaged in proscribed conduct that warrants revocation of his or her license, the licensing board may have the option of suspending the license instead of revoking it. Usually, the board will recommend suspension instead of revocation where mitigating circumstances demand leniency—for example, where a practitioner makes a misrepresentation out of ignorance as opposed to being willful. The practitioner's license is reinstated at the end of the suspension period, at which time he or she may resume practice.

HOSPITAL PRIVILEGES

Many practitioners, especially physicians and surgeons, rely on the use of hospital facilities. Generally, hospitals have newer and better equipment, facilities for overnight stays, special treatment centers for burns and other serious injuries, obstetrics, and so forth.

The staggering cost of equipping such facilities prohibits practitioners from acquiring most of this equipment for their own office or clinic use. Consequently, use of a hospital's facilities often is a necessity in order for many practitioners to provide patients the best possible treatment.

Just as a state is not obligated to grant a license to practice to anyone who requests it, neither is a hospital compelled to grant *staff privileges* to any practitioner who requests them. Nor is a hospital bound to extend privileges indefinitely once initially granted. Usually, hospitals deny or revoke staff privileges for many of the same reasons that a license to practice may be denied or revoked. Hospitals also deny or revoke privileges because the practitioner fails to follow hospital rules and regulations.

Unless a state statute provides otherwise, hospitals have the power to adopt reasonable regulations regarding the qualifications necessary for admission to practice at and use the hospitals' facilities. Such discretion is necessary in order for hospitals to maintain acceptable standards of care and protect against the risk of exposure to malpractice suits. Such discretion, if left unchecked, can be and has been abused. Therefore, some limitations have been placed on a hospital's discretion to grant, deny, and revoke staff privileges.

Generally, this discretion has been regulated by the courts rather than by statutes. The degree of discretion granted is customarily dependent upon whether the hospital is publicly or privately owned.

Public Institutions

Nonprofit hospitals (those that are publicly owned) have very little discretion in denying staff privileges. This limited discretion also applies to private hospitals that are partially funded by government funds. In the majority of states, licensed, competent practitioners may not be excluded from the use of public facilities. Such hospitals do have the right to deny or revoke staff privileges based on reasonable, nondiscriminatory grounds, such as a practitioner's prior history of incompetence or unprofessional conduct.

Private Institutions

Where a hospital has been constructed with and maintained purely by private dollars, it has a fairly broad discretion to pick and choose to whom it will extend staff privileges. Such hospitals have the right to exclude highly competent, licensed practitioners for a variety of reasons. For example, the hospital may choose to exclude a practitioner simply because of his or her field of specialty. So long as the decision to deny or revoke staff privileges is not based on unreasonable, arbitrary, or unlawful discriminatory grounds, the practitioner is left with little recourse.

In some states, both private and public hospitals may exclude all practitioners who practice a certain *system of treatment*. For example, hospital policy may dictate that no chiropractors may use hospital facilities. In other states, however, such discriminatory treatment, even though applied consistently, has been held to be illegal.

Procedural Rights

When a recommendation to revoke or deny privileges has been made, the practitioner has certain due process rights as provided in the medical staff bylaws, specifically, the right to receive notice of the charges against him or her that have culminated in the revocation or denial and the right to be heard at an informal hearing.

Practitioners who have been subject to a recommendation to have staff privileges revoked by a public hospital may have greater rights following the recommendation. The practitioner must be given notice of the pending action and the reasons therefor prior to revocation of staff privileges. In addition, the practitioner must be given a hearing and an opportunity to participate.

Fewer procedural rights may be accorded to a practitioner who has had staff privileges recommended to be revoked or denied at a private hospital. In either case, the practitioner's rights when he or she is the subject of a recommendation to revoke or deny privileges will be governed by the medical staff bylaws.

Peer Review

Peer review is the process by which a hospital's medical staff members review the quality of care administered by fellow practitioners. A peer review committee is made up of staff practitioners from the hospital and others as provided in the medical staff bylaws. Generally, each medical staff member of the hospital will undergo peer review at some point. Usually, a recommendation to revoke staff privileges is the result of a medical executive committee's investigation. The hospital's Board of Directors makes the final decision.

Where one of the peer review panel members is in direct economic competition with the practitioner whose care has been called into question, anticompetition claims are common. An example is where an ophthalmologist is being reviewed by a panel that is comprised of one or more ophthalmologists in direct economic competition.

The practitioner-hospital relationship is much more complex than this cursory discussion may lead one to believe. You should consult with a health law expert for a more in-depth analysis of the various rules, rights, and responsibilities that exist. In addition, as previously mentioned, the licensing laws vary widely from state to state. For specific details on your state's laws, check with the local chapter of your professional association. You can also find the licensing rules in your state's administrative rules or statutes.

CHAPTER 12

Patient Records and Privacy

A good record keeping system is imperative if a health care practice is to be run effectively and efficiently. Accurate, up-to-date, and orderly records are necessary for providing appropriate health care to the patient, as well as for business and legal purposes (such as managing employees, preparing income tax records, verifying payments made, and billing). In addition, federal law has made it critical to take measures to ensure the privacy of patient health care records. In this chapter and the next, we will discuss the unique issues that arise in a health care practice with respect to both health care records and business records, including the fundamentals of setting up a bookkeeping system.

HEALTH CARE RECORDS

The *health care record* is a compilation of information gathered from many sources for the general purpose of assisting the health care practitioner in providing the appropriate health care to a patient. More specifically, the *Joint Commission on Accreditation of Health Care Organizations* (JCAHO) suggests that the health care record serves several important purposes:

- it provides a basis for planning and continuity in a patient's care;

- it documents communications between the patient and the physician; and,

- it provides evidence of the course of the patient's diagnosis, condition, and treatment.

The health care record also serves important functions that are not directly related to administering care to the patient. The health care record has been referred to as the practitioner's best friend, for it provides substantive evidence of the practitioner's course of treatment and conduct with respect to a given patient for use in the defense of potential malpractice claims. In addition, if the quality of the practitioner's care is called into question by a state licensing board, a thorough health care record that details the practitioner's observations and analysis can be used to rebut a charge of incompetence or substandard care. It can also be used for medical research under certain circumstances.

There are essentially two categories of health care records, *primary* and *secondary*. The *primary record* is the original record, which is generally composed of the patient chart, X-rays, clinical test results, photographs, sketches, and the like. The *secondary record* contains information derived from the original record and is used for reimbursement and research purposes. Patient financial and billing information is also generally referred to as secondary record information. It should be noted that certain patient information—such as HIV test results and drug and alcohol abuse information—may require special treatment. These special rules will be covered in more detail later in this chapter.

CONTENT REQUIREMENTS

The actual content of the patient's health care record is a matter of professional judgment. Some states have minimum content requirements for health care records, established by law; however, minimum content requirements are generally only applicable to *health care facilities* (such as hospitals, nursing homes, and ambulatory surgical centers). A well-organized, thorough record that demonstrates a specific path of care and well-thought-out analyses is highly advised, especially in light of its evidentiary value in malpractice and competency hearings. In addition, a thorough record should enhance your ability to effectively track and diagnose a patient's particular condition.

The patient chart is one of the most important components of the health care record. The chart details the health care history of the patient and reflects the course of action with respect to particular complaints and injuries. As previously stated, content is a matter of professional judgment. It should be noted, however, that many practitioners follow the *SOAP method* of recording patients' health care histories. *SOAP* is a topical outline of what the practitioner records in his or her notes before, during, and after the office visit and stands for the following.

- Subjective description

- Objective description

- Analysis

- Proposed treatment

The *subjective description* is the patient's rendition of the injury or illness—what the patient feels, what the symptoms are, and so forth. The *objective description* is the findings after an examination of the patient. The *analysis* is just that—based on the patient's complaint and the physician's finding, it is what is believed to be wrong with the patient. Finally, the notes should record what action (if any) was taken to remedy the problem.

HIPAA

Procedures surrounding health care records and their privacy changed dramatically in 1996 with the passage of the *Health Insurance Portability and Accountability Act*, known as HIPAA. We are confident that if you are practicing medicine or another health care discipline, you have become familiar with many of the procedural requirements of HIPAA. This section is designed to give you an overview of HIPAA from a lawyer's perspective.

HIPAA is divided into two sections.

1. *Title I*, the portability provision, protects health insurance coverage for individuals (and their families) who are switching, or have been fired from, their jobs. It amends the *Employee Retirement Income Security Act* (ERISA) and the *Public Health Service Act* (PHSA).

2. *Title II* contains the *Administrative Simplification* (AS) *provisions*, which require uniform national standards for electronic health care transactions and national identifiers for any health care providers, health insurance plans, and employers. These provisions also set standards for security for the protection of the privacy of individuals' health care records and data for *electronic data interchange* (EDI). The goal of Title II is to improve efficiency in the delivery of health care services through standardization of the EDI.

Penalties for noncompliance with HIPAA include civil and criminal penalties, such as:

- fines of up to $25,000 for multiple violations of the same standard in a calendar year, and

- fines of up to $250,000 and possible imprisonment of up to ten years for misuse of identifiable patient health records.

Compliance requirements include:

- making the members of your health care organization aware of HIPAA's rules and its mission;

- assessing the organization's privacy practices, security of information systems, and procedures;

- developing a concrete action plan for compliance with each rule; and,

- developing infrastructures, both managerial and technical, to carry out the plan, which should include:

  - development of new policies, procedures, and processes that ensure privacy, security, and individual patient rights;

  - updating information systems to better safeguard personal health information;

  - training of all employees; and,

  - creating a privacy, security, and enforcement system that includes nomination of a privacy officer and a security officer.

IN PLAIN ENGLISH

Title I' s main goals are to:

- protect health insurance coverage;

- protect patients' rights concerning coverage; and,

- limit insurance provider power to limit services based on gaps in coverage.

Title II's main goals are to:

- increase the efficiency and lower the cost of transacting health care, with uniform standards nationwide, and

- protect electronic health information with security and privacy rules.

Title I of HIPAA

Title I of HIPAA prohibits any group health insurance plan or health insurance issuer from using discriminatory rules of eligibility based on:

- health status;

- physical or mental medical conditions;

- medical history;

- claims experience and prior received health care;

- genetic information; or,

- disability.

It also prohibits any group health insurance plan or health insurance issuer from requiring covered individuals to pay greater premiums than their peers based on these factors (with respect to themselves or their dependents).

HIPAA limits restrictions that a group health insurance plan can put on individuals with preexisting conditions. The plan may refuse to provide benefits for preexisting conditions for twelve months after enrollment or eighteen months after a late enrollment; however, this exclusion period may be reduced by the covered individual upon demonstration that he or she had creditable coverage before enrollment and that coverage was after any significant breaks in his or her past coverage.

Creditable coverage, broadly defined, includes nearly all individual and group health care plans, including Medicare and Medicaid. A *significant break* is defined as any consecutive sixty-three-day period without such creditable coverage. If an individual has at least eighteen months of creditable coverage without significant breaks, health care insurance providers cannot deny coverage or impose any preexisting condition exclusions on him or her.

Title II of HIPAA

The *Department of Health and Human Service*s (HHS) has drafted rules to increase the efficiency of health care systems. These rules create standards for the use and dissemination of health care data and apply to *covered entities*, which include health plans, health care clearinghouses (including billing services and community health information systems), and health care providers that transmit data and records in a way that is regulated by HIPAA. A *health care provider* is "any person or organization who furnishes, bills, or is paid for health care in the normal course of business."

The Administrative Simplification rules promulgated by the HHS consist of the following five rules.

1. Privacy Rule

2. Transactions and Code Sets Rule

3. Security Rule

4. Unique Identifiers Rule

5. Enforcement Rule

Privacy Rule and Protected Health Information

HIPAA perhaps is most notorious for its Privacy Rule, which went into effect on April 13, 2003. It established regulations for the use and disclosure of *protected health information* (PHI), which is any information about health care provision, payment for health care, or health status that can be linked to an individual patient. PHI is broadly interpreted and includes any historical data of medical records or payment history for health services.

The Privacy Rule requires that:

- all patients be informed of the health care provider's privacy practices;

- health care providers disclose any PHI to a patient within thirty days of the patient's request;

- patients be permitted to request corrections of any inaccurate information;

- *reasonable steps* be taken to ensure the confidentiality of communications with patients (for example, if required by the patient, a health care provider must call the patient's home only, instead of his or her work number);

- providers notify patients when their PHI is used for any purposes and keep tabs on PHI disclosures, privacy policies, and procedures for the medical records in question;

- all providers appoint a privacy official and contact person in charge of receiving complaints, and train their employees in regards to handling PHI; and,

- health care providers disclose only the minimum necessary amount of PHI to accomplish the intended purpose (there are exceptions, including disclosure to the patient, disclosure made pursuant to the patient's authorization, and disclosure to or requested by a health care provider for treatment purposes).

HIPAA allows providers to disclose PHI when required by law (for example, reporting potential child abuse to state welfare).

If the Privacy Rule is violated, a complaint may be filed with the Department of Health and Human Services.

Transactions and Code Sets Rule

Previously, there was a wide variety of electronic formats for health care transactions. HIPAA establishes a common standard format that improves efficiency, security standards, and simplifies the process. Adoption of these standards is mandatory unless the health care providers do not use electronic transactions. However, any organization providing health services to Medicare patients must adopt these standards because Medicare requires electronic transactions.

A good faith effort must be made to come into compliance with this rule; however, as there has been confusion and difficulty for many smaller providers in implementing this rule, penalties for noncompliance are rarely levied.

Examples of *electronic data interchanges* (EDI) are as follows.

- *Health Care Claim Transaction Set.* Information is sent from health care providers to patients, either directly or through parties such as billing services. This system is also used to transmit claims and billing information. Regulatory agencies may monitor the billing and payment of health care services within a limited field or industry, such as dentistry or chiropractic practice.

- *Health Care Claim Payment Set.* Payments are sent through this system to health care providers directly or through a financial institution. This set is also used to send an *Explanation of Benefits* (EOB).

- *Benefit Enrollment and Maintenance.* This EDI is used by employers, unions, insurance agencies, and other entities to enroll members to a payor (usually a health care organization paying claims and administering insurance benefits). Examples of payors are HMOs, PPOs, and Medicaid/Medicare, as well as any entity that can be contracted by those companies.

Health care providers are required to adopt standard code sets to be used in all health care transactions. HIPAA has promulgated coding systems and code sets for the labeling of specific diseases, injuries, and other illnesses, along with their causes, symptoms, and treatments.

Security

This rule mandates a uniform standard level of protection for health-related patient information that is stored or disseminated electronically. It requires health care providers to ensure that the protected health information that they create or receive is strictly confidential and secure. Employee and workforce compliance is necessary. No specific software or technologies are required; the security standard must merely be met by whatever solutions are chosen by each individual health care provider organization.

Unique Identifiers for Health Care Providers and Organizations

Standard identifiers are now mandatory for usage in health care business transactions between parties. An employer's tax identification number or *employer identification number* (EIN) is the standard identifier. The *National Provider Identifier* (NPI) *Rule* requires doctors, hospitals, and other health care providers to obtain and use a unique identifier when filing electronic claims with insurance providers.

Enforcement

The rule establishes proper procedures for investigations, hearings, and prosecutions of HIPAA violations. Violation of HIPAA rules results in fines and civil penalties.

Summary of HIPAA Rules and Requirements

	Privacy	Transactions and Code Sets	Security	Unique Identifiers
Purpose of Rule	Protecting patient health information	Streamlining processes to increase efficiency	Setting unifying high level of protection for patient information	Better identifying health care providers in a national system
Practical Effects	Empowering patients with respect to control and knowledge of their own health information	Setting uniform standards across health care industries	Setting a standard for safety for protected patient information	Requiring labels for all health care organizations
Required Actions	Mandating release of patient information if requested; updating as per request of patient and informing patients of disclosures	Adopting standards, if any electronic data transmissions or work with Medicare; adoption of HIPAA codes for activity, treatment, and illnesses when transmitting data between parties	Ensuring confidentiality and security with whatever solution is suitable for that company (no specific technologies required); employee participation and training	Applying for, obtaining, and continually using a unique number in all electronic claims to insurance providers
Penalties for Noncompliance	Reporting of complaint to Health and Human Services	For smaller companies, noncompliance penalties are rarely levied; "good faith" effort required	Possible fines	Corrective action is the most likely requirement

LENGTH OF RETENTION OF RECORDS

Each health care practitioner should develop a written retention policy. A good starting point for developing such a policy is to check your state's record retention requirements for health care facilities. For example, Oregon's Administrative Rules require that the following records be retained permanently in either written or computerized form:

■ patient's register (containing admissions and discharges);

■ patient's master index;

- register of all deliveries (including live births and stillbirths);

- register of all deaths;

- register of all operations;

- register of all outpatients (for seven years);

- emergency room register (for seven years); and,

- blood banking register (for twenty years).

Oregon also requires that all health care facilities' medical records be kept for at least ten years after the date of the last discharge. In addition, federal regulations require records in Medicare programs to be kept for five years after the Medicare billing report is filed.

In any event, patient records should be retained for a relatively long period of time since they may be needed to aid in litigation, such as the defense of malpractice suits. In addition, special circumstances may require that certain records be retained even longer, such as when the practitioner or patient is anticipating litigation, when there is a disputed claim, or when the practitioner is subject to an open audit period. In the celebrated *Dalkon Shield* case, for purposes of damages, claimants were required to prove their use of the contraceptive intrauterine device (IUD) through medical records that, for most, were approximately twenty years old. Generally speaking, where a retention period is not dictated by legal requirements, development of a satisfactory retention policy is a matter of meeting the practitioner's own needs.

You should have a specified procedure for the destruction of documents that are no longer necessary. Destruction of paper records is generally facilitated by shredding or incineration. Electronically stored information is erased, but you should be aware that simply deleting a file does not erase it. Discuss proper procedures with the person who handles your computer system. Destruction or erasure should either be witnessed or attested to in writing by the individual responsible for destruction or erasure to limit potential liability for negligence in handling the health care records.

SPECIAL CONFIDENTIALITY STATUTES AND CONSIDERATIONS

The federal government has promulgated special rules concerning alcohol and drug abuse patient records in addition to HIPAA. The regulations cover federally assisted programs that provide alcohol or drug abuse diagnosis, treatment, or referral for treatment. The regulations specifically define which programs and records are covered, the extent of the prohibition on disclosure, exceptions to the prohibition, and the sanctions and penalties for violation of the statute.

Most states also have special rules regarding the confidentiality and disclosure of particular types of patient information. For example, with the increasing concern over AIDS, most states have developed special confidentiality rules with respect to HIV test results. Many states also have special statutes concerning the confidentiality of mental health and developmental disability records. In addition, many states have special statutes for adoption records. These statutes, in effect, seal the court records relating to adoptions so that no one may have access to them, though a few states permit the adoptee limited access.

Maintaining confidentiality of patient information is always an issue when a health care practice is sold or permanently closed. When a practice is sold, the records are generally transferred to the new owner as part of the business. In order to facilitate a transfer that does not violate the patient's right to privacy, patients should be notified that the practice is being transferred to a new owner who will have custody of their records. A patient may decide that he or she prefers to see a practitioner other than the new owner in the future. Consequently, the notice should state that, upon the patient's written request, the records will be forwarded to any practitioner specified by the patient.

When a health care practice is closed, the patients should be notified and encouraged to find a new practitioner. The notice should inform the patients that their records will be sent to their new practitioners upon their authorization. Records that are not sent to a new practitioner should not be destroyed but should be retained by the original practitioner or the practitioner's authorized custodian, since the patient may have need for the records in the future.

Finally, special consideration should be given to the confidentiality problems inherent to a computer-based record system. Today, most practices have some, if not all, of their patient information stored on computers. Since the computer has the ability to store large quantities of information, one unauthorized entry into the system can lead to the disclosure of a tremendous amount of confidential information.

Special security systems can be installed to increase the protection of confidential information. Passwords should be used as the most basic form of protection to eliminate access by outsiders. Breaches of confidentiality are most likely to occur through the disclosure of information from an overly curious employee. Consequently, access to particularly sensitive information (such as HIV test results and drug or alcohol abuse records) should be restricted to only those who have a need and right to it. For example, the system can be installed with an alarm that sounds when an unauthorized user attempts to gain access to information beyond his or her security clearance. Discuss your options with your computer consultant.

As a prerequisite to granting access to the computer system, all individuals should be required to sign an agreement under which they promise to maintain the confidentiality of all health care information to which they gain access.

NECESSITY OF CONSENT

In most circumstances, the release of a patient's health information requires the patient's written authorization. Likewise, patient consent is an absolute defense to a claim of improper disclosure of confidential information. However, there must be proof of a written authorization verifying that the patient made a fully informed voluntary consent.

In order to be *voluntary*, the consent must be made without coercion, and the patient must have the *legal capacity* to consent. In other words, the patient must be of legal age (this varies from state to state) and of sound mind. Where the patient is a minor or is legally incompetent, the patient's parent or legal guardian must give the necessary consent for release of the information.

To ensure that the patient makes a fully informed consent, the patient must be made aware of the scope of the consent. Consequently, the authorization form should be clear and contain all the pertinent information. Federal regulations call for the following information to be on the authorization form:

- a description of the information to be used or disclosed that identifies the information in a specific and meaningful fashion;

- the name or other specific identification of the person(s), or class of persons, authorized to make the requested use or disclosure;

- the name or other specific identification of the person(s), or class of persons, to whom the covered entity may make the requested use or disclosure;

- a description of each purpose of the requested use or disclosure. The statement "at the request of the individual" is a sufficient description of the purpose when an individual initiates the authorization and does not, or elects not to, provide a statement of the purpose;

- an expiration date or an expiration event that relates to the individual or the purpose of the use or disclosure. The statement "end of the research study," "none," or similar language is sufficient if the authorization is for a use or disclosure of protected health information for research, including for the creation and maintenance of a research database or research repository; and,

■ the signature of the individual and the date. If the authorization is signed by a personal representative of the individual, a description of such representative's authority to act for the individual must also be provided.

In addition to these core elements, the authorization must contain statements adequate to place the individual on notice of all of the following:

■ the individual's right to revoke the authorization in writing;

■ the ability or inability to condition treatment, payment, enrollment, or eligibility for benefits on the authorization; and,

■ the potential for information disclosed pursuant to the authorization to be subject to redisclosure by the recipient and no longer be protected by federal privacy regulations.

Your licensing board or other professional associations may have sample forms for your use.

HIPAA requires that only the minimum disclosure necessary to fulfill the purpose stated in the authorization be made, so you must use care when determining what information to include. Other important guidelines to follow include keeping the consent form with the patient's records for future reference. The records should be marked with the statement that the records should not be released to anyone other than the person authorized by the patient. For added protection, the practitioner may want to require the recipient to sign a nondisclosure agreement.

When health records are released to third persons, a proper authorization normally is required. Common situations where consent is necessary include release to insurance companies for billing purposes, other health care providers, attorneys, and law enforcement agencies (except where compelled by law). After a patient's death, his or her health records may be obtained or released only by consent of his or her legal representatives.

In some situations, the patient's consent is not required for the release of information. Certain information is simply not considered privileged and is, therefore, subject to release without consent. *Nonprivileged information* includes such items as the patient's name and city of residence.

The most common situation where consent is not required is when an emergency necessitates release to another health care provider and the patient or legal representative is unable to give consent.

Consent is also not necessary where the law mandates disclosure of certain health information. In most states, there are certain types of information that must be reported to specific public agencies. Several examples of the many different types of information that may be required to be reported include confirmed cases of AIDS and other communicable diseases, instances of child or elder abuse and rape, unusual deaths, and workers' compensation claim information. The reporting requirements vary from state to state as to what types of cases must be reported and the manner and extent of the reports that must be filed. The practitioner who complies with the reporting requirements is granted immunity from any liability for disclosing the information.

In many states, consent is not required for the release of information to local authorities where the patient presents an immediate danger to him- or herself or another person. The practitioner must use professional judgment as to when the threat is serious enough to warrant disclosure. It should be noted, however, that courts in many states have imposed a special duty on practitioners who deal with dangerous psychiatric patients to actually breach confidentiality, following a ruling from a California court that held that a practitioner may be found civilly liable for the death of another when the practitioner knows of a patient's intention to kill or injure a particular person and fails to take appropriate steps to protect the intended victim, such as disclosing the danger to the intended victim or local authorities.

Other situations where consent is usually not required include the release of information to government payors such as Medicare or Medicaid (when necessary to secure compensation for services rendered), in response to a subpoena, and disclosure to the parents of a minor for treatment rendered to the minor.

Although HIPAA is the all-encompassing federal mandate, state law still plays a significant role with respect to many of the issues that are pertinent to health care record retention, release, and confidentiality. In light of practitioners' legal and ethical responsibilities toward patients and the consequent civil liability that flows from an improper disclosure, practitioners should check with their attorneys, licensing boards, or professional associations for further information on confidentiality and the release and retention of health records.

CHAPTER 13

Bookkeeping and Accounting

BUSINESS RECORDS AND ACCOUNTING

The purpose of any accounting system is to keep accurate records of the financial condition of the practice. A well-organized accounting system that is amenable to analysis can make encounters with the IRS less traumatic. In addition, potential creditors will look more favorably upon a professional who maintains complete records that accurately reflect the practice's fiscal condition.

Devising a satisfactory accounting system can be a rather arduous task. Although health care practitioners have considerable latitude in designing their accounting system, their freedom in this matter is not absolute. Constraints are imposed by various state and federal laws, such as tax laws, and by the *Financial Accounting Standards Board* of the *American Institute of Certified Public Accountants* (AICPA), in its regulations known as *generally accepted accounting principles* (GAAP). The law in this area, especially the federal tax law, is in a constant state of flux. In addition, it may be desirable to establish within the accounting system the necessary records to meet the needs of the practice, both for tax purposes and for business purposes.

In light of these observations and the simple fact that most health care professionals lack any formal accounting training or experience, for purposes of this chapter, we are assuming that the practitioner will hire a professional accountant to set up and maintain an accounting system. Therefore, this discussion will merely provide an introduction to some of the basic issues and terminology pertaining to accounting procedures to prepare you to ask the right questions and make well-informed decisions when you meet with your accountant.

BUSINESS YEAR

Accounting data may be arranged into monthly, quarterly, or yearly statements. Business years may be measured according to a *calendar year* or a *fiscal year*. If an organization adopts the calendar year, its business year will begin on January 1 and end on December 31. The calendar year is convenient because it corresponds to the normal time reference. Individuals, partners, and service corporations must adopt a calendar year for tax reporting. If an organization adopts the fiscal year, its business year will begin and end on the date it chooses. The fiscal year is more suitable for businesses that are engaged in seasonal activity because it allows the organization the flexibility to meet its own particular timing needs. It may also be more desirable for health care professionals who do not maintain a full-time private practice but whose primary occupation is teaching.

CASH AND ACCRUAL BOOKKEEPING METHODS

There are essentially two methods of recording income and expenses on the books: *cash* and *accrual*. In the *cash method* of accounting, all actual receipts and expenditures during a given accounting period are recorded for that period. If the practice receives and pays a $10,000 bill in Year 1, it would record both the receipt and the expense of $10,000 in Year 1. The cash method is the one preferred by most service-oriented businesses such as health care professionals, since there are usually substantial amounts of receivables that might result in tax liability prior to the actual receipt of cash under the accrual method.

The *accrual method* employs a fiction to determine receipts and expenditures in an attempt to match the income a practice receives to the expenses incurred in generating that income. Costs and expenses are recorded as they accrue, or are incurred, rather than at the time of cash payment. Income is recognized as it is realized and earned, and not at the time of collection. For example, if you perform an exam for a patient and charge that patient $100 in December 2008, but do not receive payment until January 2009, the $100 payment would be recorded for year 2008, even though you were not paid until 2009.

The accrual basis results in financial statements that recognize transactions and directly related costs at the time the transaction occurs, and other income and expenses in the period in which they accrue or are incurred and not necessarily when cash changes hands. Thus, a surgeon using the accrual method would record the receivable for an operation on the date of surgery rather than the date when payment is received. The accrual method is designed to present the fairest picture of the results of a profit-making enterprise and is thus widely used. The cash basis has the advantage of simplicity, but rarely provides a fair representation of the results of operations, because the deduction of all expenses in the year they are paid, regardless of earnings, does not accurately match expenses with income.

CURRENT AND CAPITAL EXPENDITURES

Allocation of expenses is more complicated than it may seem, however. By law, *capital expenses* must be allocated over a number of years, which in effect imposes an accrual method. Many of the expenditures necessary to maintain a health care practice are of a capital nature, as opposed to *current expenses*.

Whether an expense is identified as a capital or a current expense depends on the length of the useful life of the asset. If an item purchased is to be consumed or used up in the current accounting period (usually one year), it is characterized as a current expense for that year. Wooden tongue depressors and fluoride rinse are examples of current expenses. If the life of the asset extends into future accounting periods, its cost is a capital expense and must be spread over the useful life of the asset. For example, an X-ray machine would be depreciated for the useful life of the machine, and a prepaid insurance premium would be depreciated for the length of the policy. This means that the cost of the item must be spread over the number of years the item is expected to be in service.

Depreciation is the method by which the cost of a capital asset is recovered through yearly deductions. In theory, a capital asset is consumed over its useful life; thus the business is permitted to deduct for tax purposes a portion of the cost of the item for each year of the item's useful life. There is at least one exception to the depreciation rule—a purchaser may elect to deduct the cost of certain capital assets (up to $128,000 in 2008) in the year they are purchased and put into use, with some restrictions.

Depreciation is limited to those assets that physically lose value over time. Depreciable property includes equipment, buildings, machinery, and vehicles used in business or held for the production of income. An expenditure of $50,000 on lab equipment is recorded as a capital expense (as opposed to a current expense) because the expenditure will provide benefit in future years and thus should not be charged as an expense in the year purchased. However, such an asset, like most tangible fixed assets other than land, will not last forever; ultimately, it will have to be retired because it is physically worn out or has become inefficient or obsolete.

The method of depreciation is dependent upon when the asset was placed into service. There are numerous methods of depreciation, each of which can produce markedly different results. Most assets placed in service after 1980 and prior to 1987 are covered by a depreciation system called *Accelerated Cost Recovery System* (ACRS); for items put in service from 1987 to date, the depreciation system is called the *Modified Accelerated Cost Recovery System* (MACRS). The cost of an item of depreciable property is recoverable over a set period, depending into which one of certain specified classes it falls. For example, office furniture and equipment is considered *five-year property*, for which a statutory percentage is applied to the unadjusted cost of the property to determine the recovery deduction for each year.

An issue related to depreciation calculation is whether expenditures relating to a depreciable asset, such as improvements or repairs, should be treated as current expenses or whether they should be capitalized and added to the *basis* (cost) of the asset. Generally, if repairs or improvements arrest deterioration and appreciably prolong the life of the asset, the expenditure should be capitalized. If the expenditure involves only a minor repair, it should be treated as a current expense. In borderline cases, the decision may rest upon the tax advantage. (See Chapter 14.)

Depreciation deductions reduce the tax burden by being subtracted from the taxpayer's gross income to determine taxable income. Deductions do not result in dollar-for-dollar tax savings; that is, one dollar of deductions will not reduce taxes by one dollar. One dollar of tax credit, however, will reduce taxes by one dollar because credits are subtracted directly from the tax liability after the tax rates have been applied.

FINANCIAL STATEMENTS

Financial statements report on the status and activities of a business. They take many forms. At a minimum, a business will need an income statement and a balance sheet. In addition, you may need a statement of *owner's equity*.

IN PLAIN ENGLISH

Income Statement: Reflects profits and losses by showing earnings minus expenses over a period of time. It shows whether the business incurred a profit or loss during the given period.

Balance Sheet: Shows assets over liabilities. It shows the financial situation of the business at the time the financial statement was compiled. The residual interest is referred to as *owner's equity*.

Income Statement

The *income statement* is known by various names. It may also be called a *profit-and-loss statement*, *report on earnings*, or an *operating statement*. This statement reports the income that has been earned, the costs or expenses that have been incurred, and the net profit. It shows what has taken place in the business, from a financial standpoint, over a given accounting period.

From the various entries that comprise the statement, financial ratios can be derived. By comparing income statements to one another over several years, trends and patterns can be identified. Comparison of these income statements may infuse new meaning into the present income statement; that is, the impact of a single income statement on an observer is likely to be less important when it is considered in context. For instance, if this year's income statement discloses a lower profit margin, it may merely mean that more money was spent on new lab equipment, and future years' earnings will consequently go up. Therefore, the slight dip in profit will be less alarming.

Balance Sheet

Unlike the income statement, which reflects the financial condition of a business over an accounting period, the *balance sheet* indicates the financial position of the business at a given moment. The income statement reflects the way things were; the balance sheet reflects the way things are.

Balance sheets are composed of three basic elements: *assets*, *liabilities*, and *owner's equity*. For the sheet to balance (and the business to be considered solvent), assets must be equal to liabilities plus owner's equity.

Assets

Assets are categorized as either *current assets* or *long-term (fixed) assets*. *Current assets* are defined as assets that are likely to be consumed or subjected to change (usually converted into cash) within one year or the operating cycle of the business, whichever is larger. Current assets also include any portion of a long-term asset that may be realized within one year. Cash, accounts receivable (if collectible within one year of the statement), investments, and inventory are examples of current assets.

Long-term assets are assets used to operate a business but that are not for resale—for example, an examining table. A given asset may be either current or long-term, depending on its particular use in a given business. Long-term assets may be either tangible or intangible. *Tangible long-term assets* include property (land and office space) and equipment. These assets are usually valued at cost less allowed depreciation, where cost includes both the purchase price and any expense incurred in preparing the asset for use (for example, the cost of installing and testing a new X-ray machine).

Intangible long-term assets include such things as goodwill (if purchased as part of the business) and any patents, trademarks, or copyrights the practitioner may own. Goodwill is potentially the most valuable of intangible assets. *Goodwill* is the value of an active practice and includes the organization, trained staff, business reputation, established patients, and location, and can include lists of patients, long-term leases, and contracts. Goodwill is what makes a business sell for more than the aggregate value of its tangible assets. Goodwill cannot be recorded on the books unless one pays for it in the purchase of a practice.

Liabilities

Liabilities are also divided into current and long-term categories. *Current liabilities* are obligations due within one year. Any portion of a long-term liability that is due within one year is deemed a current liability. Current liabilities also include accounts payable (to outsiders as well as salaries to personnel), payroll taxes and benefits, accrued income taxes, and other accrued liabilities (such as short-term notes).

Long-term liabilities are obligations having a maturity date a year or more beyond the present accounting period. Long-term liabilities include mortgages, notes payable, and accounts payable.

Owner's Equity

Owner's equity plus liabilities equals assets, or, in other words, equity equals assets minus liabilities. *Owner's equity* reflects the net worth of the business.

Generally, the larger the owner's equity, the more there is available to the owner for distribution or liquidation. However, the amounts reported as owner's equity do not necessarily reveal the amounts that can reasonably be withdrawn. For the health care professional, most assets are in the form of fixed assets, such as lab and office equipment and real property, and a withdrawal of these assets would be impractical or impossible. Thus, there are certain practical and legal limitations to the amount of money that may be distributed to the owners from the owner's equity account.

IN PLAIN ENGLISH

Owner's equity is the net worth of a business. It represents assets minus liabilities. In other words, owner's equity is the residual interest that an owner has in the business once liabilities are subtracted from assets.

It often becomes necessary or desirable to establish a reserve account. Such an account may be required by law or may be established voluntarily. Reserve accounts, which diminish the amount of owner's equity available for distribution or other use, may be created for acquisition, to meet contingent liabilities, such as pending lawsuits or taxes, or to increase the capital structure of the practice.

From a creditor's viewpoint, the owner's equity represents the amount a practice can lose before the creditor's interests become jeopardized. Therefore, creditors will look to the owner's equity account to ensure that their interests are being protected by a capital cushion. Given the importance of the owner's equity, it may be desirable to account for it in a separate financial statement, particularly if the owner's equity is composed of several entries or is constantly fluctuating. An owner's equity statement should report the amount of the owner's equity at the beginning of the accounting period, the various increases and decreases that took place during the period, and the amount of the owner's equity at the end of the period.

INTANGIBLE BUSINESS CHARACTERISTICS

Income statements, balance sheets, and owner's equity statements present a financial picture of the practice, but they do not necessarily present the total picture. Two businesses having identical financial statements may have very different future prospects because of the various intangible characteristics of each one. If a practice is being examined by outsiders (such as possible lenders or purchasers of the practice), it is advantageous to include a description of these intangibles, particularly if they are favorable, as a part of the total financial report. A health care professional, for example, would want to report upon the established patient base, the quality of the trained staff and reputation of the licensed professionals, the positive relationship between the practice and its patients, the location, and so forth.

SOURCES OF INFORMATION ON ACCOUNTING

Some of the major topics of accounting procedure have been discussed here. However, the daily mechanics of the accounting process have not been considered. For this information, the health care professional can refer to various self-help bookkeeping and accounting texts, but should ultimately consult with a certified public accountant experienced in dealing with comparable practices.

CHAPTER **14**

Keeping Taxes Low

A health care practice can enhance profitability by increasing its patient services or by reducing expenses. Careful management of your practice will go far in expense reduction, but one of the most profound areas affecting business conduct is taxation. Prudent businesspeople are careful to determine the tax consequence of virtually every transaction.

Periodic meetings with your business lawyer and tax accountant in order to determine the most expeditious and cost-effective method of conducting your practice are important. At least one year-end session to evaluate business activities and tax planning is advisable.

After allowing for basic needs through personal exemptions, a narrow list of personal deductions, and one reduced tax rate at the low end of the income scale, our income tax system is essentially a fixed-rate system. There are now six graduated tax rates for individuals: 10% on the lowest taxable income range, 15%, 25%, and 28% on income in the middle taxable income ranges, and 33% and 35% on income in the highest taxable income ranges.

Long-term capital gains are taxed at a flat 15% (beginning in 2008, 0% for the taxpayers in the 10% and 15% brackets). Short-term capital gains are taxed at the same rate as your earned income. There are exceptions for gains on collectibles, which are taxed at different rates.

INCOME SPREADING

There are two important means of reducing tax liability. The first is spreading taxable income by the use of several provisions in the tax code. The second is the use of tax deductions.

INSTALLMENTS

One way a health care practice can spread income is to receive payments from patients in installments. The Internal Revenue Code (IRC) enables a taxpayer who sells property with payments received in successive tax years to report the income on an installment basis in some situations if the sale is properly structured. Under this method, tax is imposed only as payments are received. Note that this applies only to sales of property (such as medications, dietary supplements, and durable medical equipment), not services.

Care must be taken with the mechanics of this arrangement. If your patients' bills primarily are paid by the patients' health insurance plans, arrangements for structuring, if any are possible, most likely will have to be arranged with the payor. If a health care practice provides a service for a negotiable note due in full at some future date or for some other deferred-payment obligation that is essentially equivalent to cash or that has an ascertainable fair market value, the practice may have to report the total proceeds of the sale as income realized when the note is received, not when the note is paid off with cash. (A *negotiable note* is a written and signed promise to pay a specified sum of money either on demand or at a specified time, payable either to an identified party or to the bearer.)

DEFERRED PAYMENTS

Someone in a high tax bracket might wish to defer income until the future. For example, a nurse or lab technician working as an independent contractor could obtain an agreement from the employer that fees to be paid would not exceed a certain amount in any one year, with the excess to be carried over and paid in the future. This would result in tax savings if, when the deferred amounts are finally paid, the independent contractor was in a lower tax bracket.

There are drawbacks to deferred payments. First, the IRS may deem all payments to be received when the arrangement is put into place. Other risks are that the party owing the money may not be willing to pay interest on the deferred sums and the possibility that the party who owes could go broke before the debt is fully paid. One should consider these risks carefully before entering into a contract for deferred payments, because it might be quite difficult to change the arrangement if the need should arise.

SPREADING INCOME AMONG FAMILY MEMBERS

Employing Family Members

Another strategy for business owners in high tax brackets is to divert some income directly to members of their immediate families who are in lower tax brackets by hiring them as employees. Putting dependent children on the payroll can result in substantial tax savings because their salaries can be deducted as business expenses.

Your child, stepchild, sibling, or grandchild can earn up to the amount of the standard deduction without any tax liability. You as the taxpayer can still claim a personal dependency exemption for the child if:

1. the child is a U.S. citizen, resident, or national, or is a resident of Canada or Mexico;

2. the child has the same principal residence as you for more than one-half the year;

3. the child does not provide over one-half of his or her own support; and,

4. the child does not file a joint return.

This is true if the child is under 19 years of age at the end of the tax year or if the child is between the ages of 19 and 24 and is a full-time student. There is also an exception if the "child" (of any age) is permanently and totally disabled. The child may not claim a personal exemption if he or she is claimed by someone else on his or her tax return.

The following are additional restrictions on such an arrangement.

■ The salary must be reasonable in relation to the child's age and the work performed.

■ The work performed must be a necessary service to the business.

■ The work must actually be performed by the child.

Family Partnerships

A second method of transferring income to members of your family is the creation of a family partnership. Note that this option may be practical only for families with more than one health care professional in them. As noted in Chapter 1, in some states, owners of a health care entity must be licensed practitioners in the field practiced in that organization. In a family partnership, each partner receives an equal share of the overall income, unless the partnership agreement provides otherwise. The income is taxed once as individual income to each partner. Thus, if you are the parent who heads a family practice, you can break up and divert your income to your family members so it will be taxed to them according to their respective tax brackets. The income received by children may be taxed at significantly lower rates, resulting in more income reaching the family than if it had all been received by the parent, who is presumably in a higher tax bracket than the children. The law stipulates, however, that if a child is under 24 years of age and receives unearned income from the partnership, any amount over $1,700 will be taxed at the parent's highest marginal rate. This is known as the *kiddie tax.*

Although the IRS recognizes family partnerships, it may subject them to close scrutiny to ensure that such a partnership is not a sham. In addition, because partnership capital produces significant income and partners are reasonably compensated for services performed for the partnership, the IRS may opt to forbid the shift in income, in accordance with the IRC section that deals with distribution of partners' shares and family partnerships. The same section provides that a person owning a *capital interest* (or ownership interest) in a family partnership will be considered a partner for tax purposes even if he or she received the capital interest as a gift, if the gift is genuine and irrevocable.

Family Corporations and Limited Liability Companies

Some families have incorporated or created family-owned limited liability companies. Once again, as described in Chapter 1, state laws may limit ownership in these entities to licensed members of a health care profession. In addition, if the IRS questions the motivation for such incorporation, the courts will examine the intent of the family members. If the sole purpose of incorporating was tax avoidance, the scheme will not stand. If the IRS successfully contends that the business entity should be disregarded, the IRS can reallocate income from the corporation or LLC to the individual taxpayer. This will be done, for example, if the corporation or LLC does not engage in substantial business activity, does not observe proper formalities, or if its separate status is not otherwise adhered to by the businessperson.

Note that, as with partnerships, unearned income over $1,700, such as investment income on stock, is subject to the kiddie tax and will be taxed at the parent's highest marginal rate.

TAX ADVANTAGES AND DISADVANTAGES OF INCORPORATION

A C corporation or a limited liability company being taxed as a C corporation, however, may provide some tax advantages for health care professionals. As an employee, the owner can control his or her taxable income with a limited salary. Although the corporation or LLC must recognize income whenever patient services are provided and paid for, the corporation or LLC can deduct the owner's salary as well as other business expenses.

Incorporating or creating an LLC should not be done solely for tax reasons. Furthermore, since individual tax rates are now substantially lower than corporate tax rates, you may actually find that you are paying more tax on any profits left in the corporation or LLC than if you had chosen a flow-through type of entity, such as a partnership or pass-through LLC.

Additionally, there are some unavoidable legal and accounting expenses that will have to be paid for incorporation. If your practice operates on very small margins, you should determine if the possible tax savings justify the additional legal and accounting costs associated with incorporating. The cost to the entity for payroll taxes, unemployment taxes, workers' compensation, and legal and accounting fees can be substantial.

IN PLAIN ENGLISH

Use of the corporate form is no longer necessary for setting up a retirement plan. Revisions to the rules for retirement plans allow a self-employed person to set aside as much money for retirement through an SEP IRA as could be done through a corporate retirement plan.

While creating a business entity may not provide tax benefits in some situations and may even result in added expense, it still may afford you a liability shield. Many health care practices are incorporated or created as LLCs for the sole purpose of obtaining limited liability for their owners, rather than for the tax treatment accorded to business entities.

Moreover, there are several potential business tax problems that the health care professional should carefully consider before incorporating. In a C corporation, any distribution of profits to shareholders in the form of dividends will be taxed twice—once at the entity level as business income and again at the shareholder level as personal income when profits are distributed to the shareholders or owner.

This double taxation can be avoided through careful tax planning and the distribution of profits through means other than dividends, such as wages. Thus, although incorporation allows income to be shifted from the health care professional to other shareholders, such as family members, the shift may occur at the expense of double taxation without the use of careful tax planning. Obviously, it is important to consult with a certified public accountant (CPA) or tax advisor in order to determine whether the benefit of shifting income to a C corporation outweighs the effects of double taxation.

S CORPORATIONS

Another alternative for the small enterprise is to organize as an S corporation. Income from an S corporation is taxed only once, at the individual level. Although income from a partnership or sole proprietorship is also taxed only once, at the individual level, the tax rates associated with the incomes are different. In an S corporation, distributions are not subject to Social Security and Medicare taxes (FICA), though amounts paid as wages are.

LLC TAX ELECTION

The tax law allows LLCs to make an election to be taxed like a corporation or to be taxed as if the practice were still run as a sole proprietorship (in states allowing one-person LLCs) or a partnership. If no election is made, the default tax treatment will be that of a partnership, if there is more than one member, or as sole proprietorship if there is only one member. You should be aware that some states have a gross receipts tax for LLCs that may make an LLC an unattractive option in your state. (LLCs are discussed more fully in Chapter 1.)

TAXES ON ACCUMULATED EARNINGS AND PASSIVE INVESTMENT INCOME

If a person incorporates in order to postpone a significant portion of income, the IRS may impose an accumulated-earnings tax. Generally, the IRC allows a maximum accumulation of $250,000 to not be subject to the accumulated-earnings tax. However, for corporations whose principal work is in the fields of health, law, engineering, architecture, accounting, actuarial science, performing arts, or consulting, the maximum is $150,000. Accumulated earnings beyond these maximums must be justified as reasonable for the needs of the practice. Otherwise, they will be subject to a tax of 15% in addition to the regular corporate tax.

The IRC also imposes an additional tax on most types of passive investment income. Check with your accountant for more details if this may be applicable to your practice.

In addition, if the owner sells his or her stock or ownership interest before the corporation has realized any income, the corporation could become a collapsible corporation, causing the gain realized on the sale of the stock to be taxed at ordinary income rates.

QUALIFYING FOR BUSINESS DEDUCTIONS

Another means of reducing tax liability involves making use of various tax deductions. For this, you must keep full and accurate records. Receipts are a necessity. Even if your practice is home-based, you should have a separate checking account and a complete set of books for all the activities of your health care practice. Although few licensed health care professionals are likely to practice their profession as a *hobbyist*, you should be aware that if you are found to be a hobbyist, you will not be entitled to trade or business deductions, except in very limited circumstances.

Tax laws presume that a person is engaged in a business or trade, as opposed to a hobby, if a net profit results from the activity in question during three out of the five consecutive years ending with the taxable year in question. For instance, if a nurse practitioner does not have three profitable years in the last five years of working as such, the IRS may contend that the work merely constitutes a hobby. In this case, the taxpayer will have to prove profit motive in order to claim business expenses in excess of income for that year. Proof of a profit motive does not require proof that profit would actually be made. It requires proof only of intention to make a profit. If, however, the profit is nominal, the presumption may not be met.

The U.S. Department of Treasury regulations call for an objective standard on the profit-motive issue, so statements of the taxpayer as to intent will not suffice as proof. The regulations list the following nine factors to be used in determining profit motive.

1. The manner in which the taxpayer carries on the activity (i.e., effective business routines and bookkeeping procedures)

2. The expertise of the taxpayer or the taxpayer's advisors (i.e., study in an area, awards, prior publication, critical recognition, and membership in professional organizations)

3. The time and effort expended in carrying on the activity (i.e., at least several hours a day devoted to the activity, preferably on a regular basis)

4. Expectation that business assets will increase in value

5. The success of the taxpayer in similar or related activities (i.e., past successes, even if prior to the relevant five-year period)

6. History of income or losses with respect to the activity (i.e., increases in receipts from year to year, unless losses vastly exceed receipts over a long period of time)

7. The amount of occasional profits, if any, that are earned

8. Financial status (wealth sufficient to support a hobby would weigh against the profit motive)

9. Elements of personal pleasure or recreation (if significant traveling is involved and little work accomplished, the court may be suspicious of profit motive)

No single factor will determine the results.

> **EXAMPLE:** The 1928 case of *Deering v. Blair* provides an example of how the factors are used. Deering was the executor of the estate of Reginald Vanderbilt, whose financial affairs and residence were in New York. Vanderbilt had purchased a farm near Portsmouth, Rhode Island, because he was interested in horses, and operated it as a business. The business produced little income, but Vanderbilt claimed business expenses of over $25,000 in each of three years. The fact that Vanderbilt did not rely on the income from the farm for his livelihood was considered by the court in making its decision. The court held that, despite the fact that he had several employees and advertised the farm's horse-boarding and rental services, the purpose for operating the farm was not to produce a profit. Rather, the land was used for pleasure, entertaining, exhibition, and social diversion. Thus, the business deduction was disallowed.

While a new business is not presumed to be engaged in for profit until it shows a profit three out of five years, deductions have been allowed in cases where this test is not met.

EXAMPLE 1: In *Allen v. Commissioner*, the tax court decided to allow business deductions for the proprietors of a ski lodge that was rented out during the ski season. The deduction was allowed even though the lodge did not show a profit during the years in question and despite the fact that the proprietors did not depend on the income from the lodge for their livelihood. They did, however, keep accurate records and did not use the lodge for their personal pleasure. Consequently, they were able to show that the lodge was operated as a business.

EXAMPLE 2: In *Engdahl v. Commissioner*, the tax court found a profit motive on the part of the taxpayers who were considering retirement and wanted to supplement their incomes by operating a horse ranch. The court held that, despite a series of losses, the taxpayers had kept complete and accurate records reviewed by an accountant, had advertised the operation, had taken their horses to shows, and had worked up to fifty-five hours per week on the operation. Additionally, the assets of the ranch had appreciated in value. All these facts showed that the taxpayers had a profit motive and, therefore, the business-expense deductions were allowed.

Once you have established yourself as engaged in a business, all your ordinary and necessary expenditures for that business are deductible business expenses. This generally would include all the materials and supplies used in your practice, your workspace, office equipment, research or professional books and magazines, travel for business purposes, certain conference fees, any agent commissions, postage, legal fees, and accountant fees.

In past years, one of the most significant and problematic of these deductible expenses has been the workspace deduction. However, as you will see in the next section, the rules for home office deductions have relaxed in recent years. This is very important to home-based health care practitioners. The cost of renting a separate office is such that some new practitioners, especially when they are just starting up their practice, are unwilling or unable to pay it. Others, of course, choose to work at home because it enables them to juggle work and family.

Deductions for the Use of a Home in a Health Care Practice

Tax law changes have made taking a home office deduction much more attractive than it has been in the past. Each practitioner with a home-based office should consider the benefits of taking a home office deduction carefully, even if they have been told in the past that they would be better served not to take the deduction. The home office deduction allows various home expenses to be deducted against the net business income. Expenses that fall into this category include, but are not limited to:

- mortgage interest;

- real estate taxes;

- home repairs/maintenance;

- rent;

- utilities;

- insurance;

- security system; and,

- depreciation.

Indirect expenses are those that benefit both the business and the personal-use portions of the home. The business portion of the expense is taken as a percentage of the total spent. The business-use percentage is determined by dividing the square footage of business use of the home by the total square footage.

Direct expenses are those that were made to improve only the business-use portion of the home. These amounts are allowed in full.

Regularly and Exclusively

In order for use of an area of your home to be considered business use, the area must be used regularly and exclusively. *Regularly* means that the space is consistently used for business purposes, meaning that occasional use does not qualify. *Exclusively* means that the area is used only for the business purpose (there is an exception for the storage of inventory). Generally, an area is used for business if it meets these tests and is:

- the principal place of business (this includes administrative use). A home office will generally qualify as business use for administrative work if the area is used exclusively and regularly and there is no other location available for the taxpayer to conduct these activities;

- used as a place to meet clients (patients); or,

- used for business purposes and is a separate structure from the taxpayer's personal residence.

Separate Structure

When the office is in a structure separate from the principal residence, the requirements for deductibility have always been more relaxed. The structure must be used exclusively and on a regular basis, just as an office in the home. However, when the office is in a separate structure, it need only be used in connection with the business, not as the principal place of business.

Storage Areas

When taxpayers use a portion of their homes for storage of business materials (as well as for business), the requirements for deductibility of the storage areas have also been more relaxed than other rules in the recent past. The dwelling must be the sole fixed location of the business and the storage area must be used on a regular basis for the storage of the business equipment or products. The room used for storage need not be used entirely or exclusively for business, but there must be a separately identifiable space suitable for storage of the business-related materials.

> **NOTE:** No home office deductions are allowed when employees rent their homes to their employers in their capacity as employees.

Tax Advantages

The primary tax advantage comes from a deduction for an allocable portion of repairs, utility bills, and depreciation. Otherwise, these would not be deductible at all. The allocable portion is the square footage of the space used for the business, divided by the total square footage of the house, and multiplied by your mortgage interest, property taxes, etc. Determining the amount of allowable depreciation is highly complex and you should discuss it with your accountant or tax advisor.

The total amount that can be deducted for an office or storage place in the home is artificially limited. The amount that can be deducted is determined by taking the total amount of money earned in the business and subtracting the allocable portion of mortgage interest, property taxes, and other deductions allocable to the business. The remainder is the maximum amount that you can deduct for the allocable portion of repairs, utilities, and depreciation. In other words, your total business deductions in this situation cannot be greater than your total business income minus all other business expenses. The office-at-home deduction, therefore, cannot be used to create a net loss, but any disallowed home office expense can be carried forward indefinitely and deducted in future years against profits from the business.

Selling Your Home

Generally, there is an exclusion of gain of up to $250,000 ($500,000 for joint filings) on the sale of your personal residence. However, if you have taken the home office deduction, the gain may be excluded only to the extent the house was not used for business purposes. Thus, any business deductions taken for depreciation expense after May 6, 1997, will have to be recaptured and taken into income. If you plan to sell your home any time soon, you should confer with an accountant or tax advisor.

Other Professional Expenses

As mentioned earlier, deductible business expenses include not only the workspace, but also all the ordinary and necessary expenditures involved in running the health care practice. *Current expenses* (items with a useful life of less than one year) are fully deductible in the year incurred. Tongue depressors, cotton balls, office supplies, postage, and telephone bills are all examples of current expenses.

Many expenses, however, cannot be fully deducted in the year of purchase but can be depreciated. These kinds of costs are called *capital expenditures*. For example, the cost of medical and office equipment, such as an X-ray machine, ultrasound equipment, computer, word processor, or a vehicle used exclusively for the business, all of which have useful lives of more than one year, are capital expenditures and cannot be fully deducted in the year of purchase. Instead, the taxpayer must depreciate, or allocate, the cost of the item over the estimated useful life of the asset. Although the actual useful life of professional equipment will vary, fixed periods have been established in the tax code over which depreciation may be deducted.

In some cases, it may be difficult to decide whether an expense is a capital expenditure or a current expense. Repairs to machinery are one example. If you spend $500 repairing your ultrasound equipment, this expense may or may not constitute a capital expenditure. The general test focuses on whether the amount spent restoring the equipment adds to its value or substantially prolongs its useful life. Since replacing short-lived parts of a machine to keep it in efficient working condition does not substantially add to its useful life, the cost to do so would be a current cost and would be deductible. Rebuilding the equipment, on the other hand, significantly extends its useful life. Thus, such a cost is a capital expenditure and must be depreciated.

For most health care practices, an immediate deduction can be taken when equipment is purchased. In 2008, up to $128,000 of such purchases could be expensed for the year and need not be depreciated at all (though this begins to phase out when the cost of your qualifying Section 179 property placed in service in a year is more than $510,000).

Fees paid to staff members, lawyers, or accountants for business purposes are generally deductible as current expenses. The same is true of salaries paid to others whose services are necessary for the business.

IN PLAIN ENGLISH

If you need to hire occasional help, it is a good idea to hire people on an individual project basis as independent contractors rather than as regular employees. This avoids your having to pay Social Security, disability, and withholding-tax payments on their accounts. You should specify the job-by-job basis of the assignments, detail when each project is to be completed, and, if possible, allow the person you are hiring to choose the place to do the work. If there is any doubt about whether an individual is actually an independent contractor, contact a skilled employment law attorney, since the IRS could characterize the individual as an employee. In that event, you will be responsible for tax withholding and paying FICA taxes.

Travel Expenses

On a business trip, whether within the United States or abroad, your ordinary and necessary expenses, including travel and lodging, may be 100% deductible if your travel is solely for business purposes (except for luxury water travel). Business meals and meals consumed while on a business trip are deductible up to 50% of the actual cost. If the trip primarily involves a personal vacation, you can deduct business-related expenses at the destination, but you may not deduct the transportation costs.

If the trip is primarily for business, but part of the time is given to a personal vacation, you must indicate which expenses are for business and which are for pleasure. In such cases, a portion of the business-related expenses will be nondeductible. This is not true in the case of foreign trips if one of the following exceptions applies.

■ You had no substantial control over arranging the trip.

■ Less than 25% of the time was spent in nonbusiness activity.

■ The trip outside the United States was for a week or less.

■ A personal vacation was not a major consideration in making the trip.

If you are claiming one of these exceptions, you should be careful to have supporting documentation. If you cannot take advantage of one of the exceptions, you must allocate expenses for the trip abroad according to the percentage of the trip devoted to business as opposed to vacation.

Determining Business Stay
The definition of what constitutes a business stay can be very helpful to the taxpayer in determining a trip's deductibility. Travel days, including the day of departure and the day of return, count as business days if travel outside the United States is for more than seven days and business activities occurred on such days. Any day that the taxpayer spends on business counts as a business day, even if only a part of the day is spent on business. A day in which business is canceled through no fault of the taxpayer counts as a business day. Saturdays, Sundays, and holidays count as business days even though no business is conducted, provided that business is conducted on the Friday before and the Monday after the weekend, or on one day on either side of the holiday.

Entertainment Expenses
Depending on the nature of your health care practice, you may incur entertainment expenses in the course of operating or developing your practice.

Entertainment expenses incurred for the purpose of developing an existing practice are deductible in the amount of 50% of the actual cost. However, you must be especially careful about recording entertainment expenses. You should record in your logbook the amount, date, place, type of entertainment, business purpose, substance of the discussion, the participants in the discussion, and the professional or business relationship of the parties who are being entertained. Make sure to save all receipts for any expenses over seventy-five dollars. You should also keep in mind the stipulation in the tax code that disallows deductibility for expenses that are lavish or extravagant under the circumstances. No guidelines have yet been developed as to the definition of the terms *lavish* or *extravagant*, but one should be aware of the restriction nevertheless. If tickets to a sporting, cultural, or other entertainment event are purchased, only the face value of the ticket is allowed as a deduction. If a skybox or other luxury box seat is purchased or leased and is used for business entertaining, the maximum deduction now allowed is 50% of the cost of a nonluxury box seat.

Conventions

The rules for business travel and entertainment expenses are more stringent when incurred while attending conventions and conferences outside the United States. Also, the IRS tends to review very carefully any deductions for attendance at business seminars that also involve a family vacation, whether inside the United States or abroad. In order to deduct the business expense, the taxpayer must be able to show, with documents, that the reason for attending the meeting was to promote production of income. Normally, for a spouse's expenses to be deductible, the spouse must be a co-owner or employee of the business.

IN PLAIN ENGLISH

Seminars often offer special activities for husbands and wives and will provide necessary documentation at a later date.

As a general rule, the business deductions are allowed for conventions and seminars held in North America. The IRS is taking a closer look at cruise ship seminars and is requiring two statements to be attached to the tax return. The first statement substantiates the number of days on the ship, the number of hours spent each day on business, and the activities in the program. The second statement must come from the sponsor of the convention to verify the initial information. In addition, the ship must be registered in the United States and all ports of call must be located in the United States or its possessions. The deduction is also limited to $2,000 per individual per year. Again, the key for the taxpayer taking this sort of deduction is careful documentation and substantiation.

Logbooks

Keeping a logbook or expense diary is probably the best line of defense for the health care professional with respect to business expenses incurred while traveling. If you are on the road, keep the following in mind.

- With respect to travel expenses:

  - keep proof of the costs;

  - record the time of departure;

  - record the number of days spent on business; and,

  - list the places visited and the business purposes of your activities.

- With respect to the transportation costs:

- keep copies of all receipts in excess of seventy-five dollars;

- if traveling by car, keep track of mileage; and,

- log all other expenses in your diary.

Similarly, with meals, tips, and lodging, keep receipts for all items over seventy-five dollars, and make sure to record all less expensive items in your logbook.

Professionals may also take tax deductions for their attendance at workshops, seminars, retreats, and the like, provided they are careful to document the business nature of the trip. Accurate record keeping is the first line of defense for tax preparation.

> **NOTE:** It is no longer possible to deduct for investment seminars or conventions, as opposed to business conventions.

CHARITABLE DEDUCTIONS

The law provides that an individual or business can donate either money or property to qualified charities and take a tax deduction for the donation. Individuals are afforded more favorable deductions for donations of money or property they own than are artists donating their creations or businesspeople who donate property out of their inventories. Note that there is no deduction allowed for the donation of services. Thus, you could deduct the cost of donated flu vaccine, but you could not deduct the value of your time spent giving the flu shots.

The tax law requires independent appraisals of property donated in a form prescribed in the IRC. In addition, if the taxpayer receives any benefit from the charity, the amount deducted must be reduced by the fair market value of the benefit received. Benefits could include, for example, attendance at museum openings or merchandise such as books, tapes, or CDs.

Since this area can be quite technical, you should consult with your tax advisor before making any charitable donations. In addition, there have been some abuses on the part of charities that resulted in misappropriations of donated funds. If you have any question about the validity of a particular charity, you should contact your state attorney general's office or the local governmental agency that polices charitable solicitations in your area.

GRANTS, PRIZES, AND AWARDS

Individuals who receive income from grants or fellowships should be aware that this income can be excluded from gross income and thus represents considerable tax savings. For an individual to qualify for this exclusion, the grant must be for the purpose of furthering his or her education and training. However, amounts received under a grant or fellowship that are specifically designated to cover expenses related to the grant are no longer fully deductible. Furthermore, if the grant is given as compensation for services or is primarily for the benefit of the grant-giving organization, it cannot be excluded.

For scholarships and fellowships granted after August 16, 1986, the deduction is allowed only if the recipient is a degree candidate. The amount of the exclusion from income is limited to the amounts used for tuition, fees, books, supplies, and equipment. Amounts designated for room, board, and other incidental expenses are included in income. No exclusion from income is allowed for recipients who are not degree candidates.

These rules apply to income from grants and fellowships. Unfortunately, the *Tax Reform Act of 1986* also put tighter restrictions on money, goods, or services received as prizes or awards. Previously, the amounts received for certain awards were excluded from income if the recipient was rewarded for past achievements and had not applied for the award. Examples of this type of award are the Pulitzer Prize and the Nobel Prize. Under the present law, any prizes or awards for religious, charitable, scientific, or artistic achievements are included as income to the recipient unless the prize is assigned to charity.

HEALTH INSURANCE

As noted earlier, business entities may deduct the cost of health insurance provided to employees, as well as to their spouses and dependents. Self-employed individuals also may deduct the amount paid for health insurance for themselves, their spouses, and their dependents.

Another tax-savings device is the *Health Savings Account*, which allows an employer to deduct amounts placed in the employee Health Savings Account, although the employee is not taxed on withdrawals made for health expenses. There are, of course, restrictions you should discuss with your benefits advisor.

IN PLAIN ENGLISH

If you do not know whether a particular activity is deductible, consult with a competent CPA or tax advisor. In any case, consultation with qualified tax professionals is always advisable to ensure maximum benefits.

CHAPTER 15

Retirement Plans

One of the methods by which a health care professional may attract and retain key personnel is to provide certain benefits. Today, one of the most important benefits for employees is the ability to participate in a retirement plan. In addition, any form of succession planning will necessitate the establishment of a method by which the senior generation can step down and hand off control of the business. In order to create an effective succession plan, it is necessary to implement an arrangement that provides an economic incentive for senior workers to retire. This is likely to be a retirement plan.

A *retirement plan* is a written savings program. If the plan meets specific rules and regulations, then it is called a *qualified plan*. This means contributions are tax deductible for the person or the business making the investments. Income taxes on the investment earnings are delayed until benefits are paid to participants. A qualified plan is one of the last remaining legal tax shelters available to highly compensated individuals. It may be used to set aside funds for retirement and to attract and retain key employees. If properly structured and invested on a prudent basis with a diversified portfolio of investments, the plan should provide financial security for the individual's retirement.

Since 1982, federal tax laws have allowed unincorporated businesses the same status as corporations with regard to qualified retirement plans. Furthermore, this same legislation eliminated the need for a corporate trustee (who was approved by the IRS), thus allowing the self-employed person the very practical advantage of being the trustee of his or her own plan.

IN PLAIN ENGLISH

When choosing a plan, select the type that will most satisfactorily meet your needs and those of your employees.

There are essentially two types of qualified plans—*defined benefit* and *defined contribution*.

DEFINED BENEFIT PLANS

Contributions to a *defined benefit plan* are determined by a relatively complex formula and are then monitored by an enrolled actuary. The promised benefit is not to exceed the lesser of 100% of the employee's annual average income for the three highest-salaried consecutive years or a specified amount that is adjusted annually and dependent on changes in the Consumer Price Index. The amount is $185,000 in 2008; for other years, see the IRS website at **www.irs.gov**. *Excess earnings* (investment income greater than the assumptions made by the actuary) are used to reduce the cost of contributions to the plan by the employer.

Advantages

Normally, defined benefit plans are appropriate where the practitioner is mature, with less than ten to fifteen working years until retirement. Defined benefit plans are appropriate—and potentially beneficial—for practices that have enjoyed considerable financial success with limited fluctuations in cash flow. The defined benefit plan can be designed to drain excess funds and allocate them to retirement on behalf of the senior preferred participant (the principal owner). In many instances, this same advantage can be attained through the use of an age-weighted defined contribution plan, such as a profit-sharing or target-benefit plan.

DEFINED CONTRIBUTION PLANS

In a *defined contribution plan*, the contribution on behalf of the participant is defined and is usually either a discretionary amount or a percentage of his or her annual compensation (ignoring compensation in excess of $230,000 in the 2008 tax year). The benefit that will be available to the participant at retirement is not defined. Investment earnings increase the retirement benefit for the plan participants, and the longer the period over which investments are accumulated and interest is earned, the greater the amount of benefits that will be available to the participants at retirement.

IN PLAIN ENGLISH

A major difference between a defined contribution plan and a defined benefit plan is who bears the risk of poor investment performance. The employer bears the risk in defined benefit plans, whereas participants bear this risk in defined contribution plans.

Profit-sharing plans, money-purchase plans, and salary savings or reduction plans, such as 401(k)s and SIMPLE plans, are all defined contribution plans, as are *Simplified Employee Pension Plans* (SEPs) and *Employee Stock Ownership Plans* (ESOPs). Note that some of those plans are group plans designed for all employees of your practice, whereas others (such as IRAs and Roth IRAs) are for you (or your employees) personally.

PROFIT-SHARING PLANS

If the income from your practice varies significantly from year to year, a profit-sharing plan may be the most appropriate type of plan to offer your employees. Contributions may be determined at or after the end of the tax year. Contributions to the plan can be determined a vote of your business's management. It is no longer required that business entities, such as corporations or certain types of LLCs, actually have a profit in order to make a contribution. The maximum deductible contribution to a profit-sharing plan is now 25% of a participant's annual compensation, with each participant's total annual addition limited to $46,000 per year.

SALARY SAVINGS/REDUCTION PLANS

These plans, which include 401(k)s, are a variant of profit-sharing plans. Under this type of plan, the employee elects to have a percentage of his or her gross salary diverted into a qualified plan. Employees can have a choice of saving on a tax-deferred basis or by making after-tax Roth contributions that may eventually qualify for tax-free withdrawal. Depending on the plan, the employer may elect to match all or a portion of the contributions made by the employee.

The main feature of salary savings/reduction plans is that a portion of the cost shifts from the employer to the employee. The business, therefore, makes less of a cash contribution.

A potential drawback is the limitation of contributions by highly compensated employees. The maximum contributions allowable continuously change and can be found on the IRS website at **www.irs.gov**. In addition, owners and highly compensated employees may not be allowed to save the maximum amount if the savings rate of the other employees is too low. They are generally allowed to save about 2% more of compensation than the average of the nonhighly compensated employees. To avoid being limited by this restriction, you may consider a safe harbor 401(k) plan that requires advance notice to participants and a nonforfeitable employer contribution.

A new approach to dealing with low savings rates of rank-and-file employees is called *automatic enrollment*. Instead of being asked how much they want to save, they are informed that they will be saving at a plan-prescribed rate unless they elect otherwise. A year later, the plan's *automatic escalation* feature kicks in to raise their savings rate unless they act. Studies have proven that this inertia approach increases the overall savings rate substantially.

SIMPLIFIED EMPLOYEE PENSION PLANS

These plans are often viewed incorrectly as an alternative to the more highly structured qualified plans. The maximum contribution that the employer may contribute per participant to an SEP continues to change and can be found on the IRS website at **www.irs.gov**. Contributions are based on an equal percentage of annual salary for all employees 21 years or older who have performed service for the employer during at least three out of five years. Although its low maintenance cost is an initial attraction, its simplicity results in a significant inflexibility that many employers are not willing to accept. For example, those whose employment has been terminated must share in any contribution, and all contributions are 100% vested and non-forfeitable.

SIMPLE IRAS

SAR/SEPs (Salary Reduction Simplified Employee Pension plans) could no longer be created after December 31, 1996. Existing SAR/SEPs were grandfathered in and are allowed to exist until the employer terminates them. A new salary reduction plan called the SIMPLE IRA was introduced to replace the SAR/SEP. This plan is available to employers with up to one hundred employees. Employees are eligible if they earned at least $5,000 during any of the previous two years and are expected to earn at least $5,000 during the current year. These requirements can be reduced or eliminated if the employer waives them. The maximum employee contribution for 2008 is $10,500 for participants under the age of 50 and $13,000 for participants aged 50 or older.

The employer is required to match up to 3% of the employee's compensation. Vesting for the employer contributions is 100% and immediate.

MONEY-PURCHASE PLANS

This type of defined contribution plan has a fixed funding requirement, such as 10% of the compensation of all eligible participants. It also requires that participants be offered a qualified joint and survivor annuity (either 50% or 75%) as a form of benefit distribution. It has the same tax deduction and annual addition limits that apply to profit-sharing plans. Most new plan sponsors choose the profit-sharing plan instead. Many money-purchase plans have been converted to profit-sharing plans.

EMPLOYEE STOCK OWNERSHIP PLANS

In an Employee Stock Ownership Plan (ESOP), the majority of the assets are shares of stock in the corporate plan sponsor. Generally, ESOPs are not useful for owners of small businesses. This plan will not be available for corporations whose shareholders must be licensed for the type of health care they are providing if any of the employees are not so licensed.

HYBRID PLANS

The *target-benefit plan* is receiving renewed interest as a result of changes in income tax law. This hybrid plan combines the contribution and benefit levels of a defined contribution plan with the recognition for mature employees found in a defined benefit plan. Another hybrid, the *age-weighted profit-sharing plan* (AWPSP), is also available. As with the target-benefit plan, the contributions are weighted or skewed toward senior employees.

DESIGNING AND DOCUMENTING A PLAN

The creation of a qualified plan requires the creation and adoption of a written plan document and trust agreement before the end of the first plan year. A summary plan description must also be drafted to inform participants about the plan. Documentation is available in two forms—*prototype documents* and *individually-drafted documents*. Each form has its own advantages and limitations. It is, therefore, essential to work with an experienced professional when selecting and establishing a plan.

EMPLOYER-SPONSORED PLANS

Many qualified plans of small businesses are *top heavy*. This is a special status that results from key employees having more than 60% of the plan's benefits. As a result, minimum contribution rules apply. The minimum contribution is the lesser of 3% of compensation or the highest rate allocated to a key employee.

Plans may be combined or stacked in order to more specifically meet the needs of the business. However, this creates a need for separate sets of rules and limitations. Stacking also increases the amount of administrative paperwork and forms, thus driving up the cost of operating and maintaining the plan. Fortunately, the need to stack plans was significantly reduced in 2002, when the deduction limit of profit-sharing plans was raised from 15% to 25%.

The following outlined design features can be used to limit or reduce the cost of rank-and-file employees in the employer-sponsored plan.

Vesting

A key element of any qualified plan is rewarding long-term service by employees. One method used to limit benefits for employees who have been employed for a relatively short period of time is a vesting schedule that forfeits all or some of the participant's employer-provided benefits. *Vesting* means having rights in, i.e., the employee has the right to all or part of his or her benefits in the retirement plan.

Currently, there are two alternative statutory vesting schedules.

1. *Three-year cliff vesting.* This schedule does not allow vesting for employees with less than three years of service. Upon completion of three years of service, the employee is 100% vested in all employer-provided benefits.

2. *Two-to-six-year graded vesting.* This vesting schedule provides for 20% vesting after two years of employment and an additional 20% for each subsequent year. After completing six years of employment, the employee is eligible to receive 100% of the employer-provided benefits upon termination of employment.

Minimum Hours

The plan sponsor may exclude employees from participation until they have been paid for at least one thousand hours during a twelve-month period. In addition, each year's contribution can be limited to those participants who are paid for at least five hundred hours. These minimum-hour features can be useful for businesses that use temporary or part-time employees.

Minimum Age

The plan sponsor may also limit participation of employees through the use of a minimum-age requirement. Current law allows an employer to postpone participation by employees under 21 years of age. At the time the employee reaches age 21, he or she enters the plan and all his or her years of employment are counted in the vesting formula.

Unions

Employees that are part of a collective bargaining unit may be specifically excluded from participation in a qualified plan established by an employer for its nonunion employees, provided that retirement benefits were the subject of good faith bargaining.

Integration with Social Security

This feature allows the plan sponsor to recognize contributions made on behalf of the employee to Social Security. An *integrated plan* (also referred to as *allowing permitted disparity*) has an extra contribution for those whose compensation is greater than the Social Security wage base ($102,000 in 2008).

INVESTMENTS IN A QUALIFIED PLAN

The primary governing law regarding investments made by a qualified plan comes from the *Employee Retirement Income Security Act* (ERISA). Under its *Prudent Expert Investment Principle*, investments should be made with primary consideration given to what an expert, rather than an amateur, investor would do.

There is a plethora of investment opportunities, including stocks, bonds, money market accounts, real estate, and partnership interests. It is, therefore, essential for you to confer with a registered investment advisor or certified financial planner to structure your plan investments based on the plan's goals, the economy, and other relevant factors.

CHAPTER 16

Estate Planning

No matter what manner of health care practice you are involved with and no matter how successful you are in that practice, the time that you will work with your practice is limited by either retirement or death. Prudent professionals will make appropriate plans for both. This is commonly known as *succession planning*. One of the most important aspects of succession planning is *estate planning*. (Another aspect of succession planning is retirement, discussed in Chapter 15.)

All health care professionals should give some thought to estate planning and take the time to execute a proper will. Without a will, there is simply no way to control the disposition of one's property. Sound estate planning may include transfers outside the will, since these types of arrangements typically escape the delays and expenses of probate. These might include *payable on death* accounts and owning real property with the right of survivorship. Certain types of trusts can be valuable will substitutes but they may be subject to challenge by a surviving spouse.

Proper estate planning will require the assistance of a knowledgeable lawyer and, perhaps, also a life insurance agent, an accountant, a real estate agent, and a bank trust officer. What help will be needed and from whom will depend on the nature and size of the estate. This chapter considers the basic principles of estate planning.

This discussion is not a substitute for the aid of a lawyer experienced in estate planning; rather, it is intended to introduce you to the basic principles, alert you to potential problems, and aid in preparing you to work with your estate planner.

THE WILL

A will is a legal instrument by which a person directs the distribution of property in his or her estate upon death. The maker of the will is called the *testator*. Recipients of gifts are known as *beneficiaries* or *legatees*. Gifts given by a will are referred to as *bequests* (personal property) or *devises* (real estate).

Certain formalities are required by state law to create a valid will. About half the states require formally witnessed wills—that is, that the instrument be in writing and signed by the testator in the presence of two or more witnesses. The other states allow either witnessed or holographic wills. A will that is entirely handwritten and signed by the testator is known as a *holographic will*.

A will is a unique document in two respects. First, if properly drafted, it is *ambulatory*, meaning it can accommodate change, such as applying to property acquired after the will is made. Second, a will is *revocable*, meaning that the testator has the power to change or cancel it at any time. Even if a testator makes a valid agreement not to revoke the will, the power to revoke it remains, though a testator who uses that power may be liable for breach of contract.

Generally, courts do not consider a will to have been revoked unless it can be established that the testator either:

1. performed a physical act of revocation, such as burning or tearing up a will with intent to revoke it; or,

2. later executed a valid will that revoked the previous will.

Most state statutes also provide for automatic revocation of a will, in whole or in part, if the testator is subsequently divorced or married.

To change a will, the testator must execute a supplement, known as a *codicil*. It has the same formal requirements as those for creating a will. To the extent that the codicil contradicts the will, the contradicted parts of the will are revoked.

Payment of Testator's Debts

When the testator's estate is insufficient to satisfy all the bequests in the will after debts and taxes have been paid, some or all of the bequests in the will must be reduced or even eliminated entirely. The process of reducing or eliminating bequests is known as *abatement*. The priorities for reduction are set by state law according to the category of each bequest. The legally significant categories of gifts are generally as follows:

- *specific bequests or devises*, meaning gifts of identifiable items (I give X all the furniture in my home);

- *demonstrative bequests or devises*, meaning gifts that are to be paid out of a specified source unless that source contains insufficient funds, in which case the gifts will be paid out of the general assets (I give Y $1,000 to be paid from my shares of stock in ABC Corporation);

- *general bequests*, meaning gifts to be paid out of the general assets of an estate (I give Z $1,000); and,

- *residuary bequests or devises*, meaning gifts of whatever is left in the estate after all other gifts and expenses are satisfied (I give the rest, residue, and remainder of my estate to Z).

Intestate property (property not governed by a will but part of the testator's estate) is usually the first to be taken to satisfy claims against the estate. (If the will contains a valid residuary clause, there will be no such property.) Next, residuary bequests will be taken. If more money is needed, general bequests will be taken, and, lastly, specific and demonstrative bequests will be taken together in proportion to their value. Some states, however, provide that all gifts, regardless of type, abate proportionately.

Disposition of Property Not Willed

If the testator acquires more property during the time between signing the will and death, the disposition of such property will also be governed by the will. If such property falls within the description of an existing category in the will (i.e., I give all my stock to X; I give all my real estate to Y), it will pass along with all similar property. If it does not and the will contains a valid residuary clause, such after-acquired property will go to the residuary legatees. If there is no residuary clause, such property will pass outside the will to the persons specified in the state's law of intestate succession.

INTESTATE SUCCESSION

When a person dies without leaving a valid will, this is known as *dying intestate*. The estate of a person who dies intestate is distributed according to the state law of *intestate succession*. These laws specify who is entitled to what parts of the estate. In general, intestate property passes to those persons having the nearest degree of kinship to the decedent. An intestate's surviving spouse will always receive a share, generally at least one-third of the estate. An intestate's surviving children generally get a share. If some of the children do not survive the intestate, the grandchildren of the intestate may be entitled to a share by representation.

Representation is a legal principle meaning that if an heir does not survive the intestate but has a child who does survive, that child will represent the nonsurviving heir and receive that parent's share in the estate. In other words, the surviving child stands in the shoes of a dead parent in order to inherit from a grandparent who dies intestate.

If there are no direct descendants surviving, the intestate's surviving spouse will take the entire estate or share it with the intestate's parents. If there is neither a surviving spouse nor any surviving direct descendant of the intestate, the estate will be distributed to the intestate's parents or, if the parents are not surviving, to the intestate's siblings by representation. If there are no surviving persons in any of these categories, the estate will go to surviving grandparents and their direct descendants. In this way, the family tree is constantly expanded in search of surviving relatives.

If none of the persons specified in the law of intestate succession survive the testator, the intestate's property ultimately goes to the state. This is known as *escheat*.

The laws of intestate succession make no provision for friends, in-laws, or stepchildren. Children adopted by the testator are treated the same as natural children for all purposes.

Note that while these guidelines apply in most states, there are different intestate schemes in states with community (or quasi-community) property laws. You should, therefore, consult with an estate planning attorney regarding intestate succession in your own state.

SPOUSE'S ELECTIVE SHARE

State law will often provide a testator's surviving spouse with certain benefits from the estate even if the spouse is left out of the testator's will. Historically, these benefits were known as *dower* in the case of a surviving wife, or *curtesy* in the case of a surviving husband. In place of the old dower and curtesy, modern statutes give the surviving spouse the right to elect against the will and, thereby, receive a share equal to at least one-fourth of the estate. Here again, state laws vary. In some states, the surviving spouse's elective share is one-third. The historical concepts of dower and curtesy are in large part a result of the law's traditional recognition of an absolute duty on the part of the husband to provide for the wife. Modern laws are perhaps better justified by the notion that most property in a marriage should be shared because the financial success of either partner is due to the efforts of both.

ADVANTAGES OF HAVING A WILL

A will affords the opportunity to direct the distribution of one's property and to set limitations by making gifts conditional. For example, if an individual wishes to donate certain property to a specific charity, but only if certain conditions are adhered to, a will can make such conditions a prerequisite to the donation.

A will permits the testator to nominate an *executor*, called a *personal representative* in some states, to watch over and administer the estate in accordance with the testator's wishes and the law of the state where the will is being handled. If no executor is named in the will, the court will appoint one. A will permits the testator to give property to minors and to regulate the timing and uses of the property given (i.e., funds to be used exclusively for education).

If the testator has unusual types of property, such as antiques, artwork, publishable manuscripts, or intangibles, such as copyrights, trademarks, patents, and the like, it is a good idea to appoint joint executors, one with financial expertise and the other with expertise in valuation in the genre in question. If joint executors are used, some provision should be made in the will for resolving any deadlock between the two. For example, a neutral third party might be appointed as an arbitrator who is directed to resolve any impasses after hearing both sides.

It is also advisable to define the scope of the executor's power by detailed instructions. A lawyer's help will be necessary to set forth all of these important considerations in legally enforceable, unambiguous terms. It is essential in a will to avoid careless language that might be subject to attack by survivors unhappy with the will's provisions. A lawyer's assistance is also crucial to avoid making bequests that are not legally enforceable because they are contrary to public policy (e.g., if an individual gets married after signing his or her will, a bequest to someone other than the new spouse will fail).

ADVANCE DIRECTIVES (LIVING WILLS) AND OTHER ESTATE PLANNING DOCUMENTS

An *advance directive* describes the kind of care you would like to have if you become unable to make medical decisions. It also allows you to appoint a representative who will oversee your health care. You may indicate that you wish to leave certain decisions to the wisdom of your representative, or you may set forth directions for your representative to follow.

Each state has its own laws regarding health care directives, and most states require particular language and supply standard forms.

A health care power of attorney is not a general power of attorney and does not give your health care representative control over your finances or possessions. It will become effective only if you are medically incapable of making decisions for yourself.

Note that if you wish to have a personal representative available to take care of nonmedical concerns while you are medically incapacitated, you should execute a special or general power of attorney.

ESTATE TAXES

In addition to giving the testator significant posthumous control over division of property, a carefully drafted will can greatly reduce the overall amount of estate tax paid at death. The following information on taxing structures relates to federal estate taxation. State estate tax laws often contain similar provisions, but state law must always be consulted for specifics.

Gross Estate

The first step in evaluating an estate for tax purposes is to determine the *gross estate*. The gross estate will include all property over which the deceased had significant control at the time of death. In addition to certain bank accounts, examples would include properly held residences, investments that have been structured to avoid probate, certain life insurance proceeds and annuities, jointly held interests, and revocable transfers.

Under current tax laws, the executor of an estate may elect to value the property in the estate either as of the date of death or as of a date six months after death. The estate property must be valued in its entirety at the time chosen. However, if the executor elects to value the estate six months after death and certain pieces of property are distributed or sold before then, that property will be valued as of the date of distribution or sale.

Valuation

Fair market value is defined as the price at which property would change hands between a willing buyer and a willing seller when both buyer and seller have reasonable knowledge of all relevant facts. Such a determination is often very difficult to make, especially when items such as a nonpublicly-traded business, artwork, antiques, other collectibles, and intangibles such as intellectual property are involved. Although the initial determination of fair market value is generally made by the executor when the estate tax return is filed, the Internal Revenue Service may disagree with the executor's valuation and assign assets a much higher or lower fair market value.

When an executor and the IRS disagree with regard to valuation, the court will decide the matter. In most cases, the burden will be on the taxpayer to prove the value of the asset. Thus, expert testimony and evidence of the sale of the same or similar properties will be helpful. In general, courts are reluctant to determine valuation by formula.

The Taxable Estate

Figuring the taxable estate is the second major step in evaluating an estate for tax purposes, after determining the gross estate. The law allows a number of deductions from the gross estate in determining the amount of the taxable estate. The *taxable estate* is the basis upon which the tax owing is computed. A discussion of some of the key deductions used to arrive at the amount of the taxable estate follows.

Typical deductions from the gross estate include funeral expenses, certain estate administration expenses, debts and enforceable claims against the estate, mortgages and liens, and, perhaps most significant, the marital deduction and the charitable deduction.

Marital Deduction

The *marital deduction* allows the total value of any interest in property that passes from the decedent to the surviving spouse to be subtracted from the value of the gross estate. The government will eventually get its tax on this property when the spouse dies, but only to the extent such interest is included in the spouse's gross estate. The spouse, of course, may limit or eliminate the estate tax on his or her estate by implementing certain estate-planning procedures. This deduction may occur even in the absence of a will making a gift to the surviving spouse, since state law generally provides that the spouse is entitled to at least one-fourth of the overall estate regardless of the provisions of the will.

Charitable Deduction

The *charitable deduction* refers to the tax deduction allowed upon the transfer of property from an estate to a recognized charity. Since the definition of a *charity* for tax purposes is quite technical, it is advisable to insert a clause in the will providing that if the institution specified to receive the donation does not qualify for the charitable deduction, the bequest shall go to a substitute qualified institution at the choice of the executor.

Exclusion

Tax credits result in an exemption that is available to every estate. For tax year 2008, the exclusion amount is $2 million; in tax year 2009, the exclusion amount is $3.5 million. That is, the estate of a person dying in 2008 with a taxable estate of $2 million would not owe any estate tax. There is also an additional exemption for families with qualifying businesses or farms.

Calculating the Tax

Deductions and the exclusion amount are subtracted from the gross estate to arrive at the taxable estate. The taxable estate is taxed at the rate specified by the *Unified Estate and Gift Tax Schedule*. The unified tax imposes the same rate of tax on gifts made by will as on gifts made during life. It is a *progressive tax*, meaning the percent paid in taxes increases with the amount of property involved.

The rates rise significantly for larger estates. For example, the rate increases from 15%, where the cumulative total of taxable estate and taxable gifts is under $10,000, to 45%, where the cumulative total is over $2 million. Federal estate tax is also reduced by the state death tax credit or the actual state death tax, whichever is less.

Paying the Tax

The deductions and exclusions previously discussed allow most estates to escape paying estate taxes altogether. For those estates with estate taxes due, generally, estate taxes must be paid when the estate tax return is filed (within nine months of the date of death). Arrangements may be made to spread payments out over a number of years, if necessary.

IN PLAIN ENGLISH

It is not uncommon for executors to be forced to sell properties for less than full value in order to pay taxes. This can be avoided by obtaining insurance policies, the proceeds of which can be set up in a trust. (See the "Trusts" section of this chapter for more information.)

DISTRIBUTING PROPERTY OUTSIDE THE WILL

Property can be distributed outside the will by making *inter vivos* gifts (given during the giver's lifetime), either outright or by placing the property in an irrevocable trust prior to death.

Advantages

A potential advantage to distributing property outside the will is that the property escapes the delays and expense of *probate*, the court procedure by which a will is validated and administered. In the past, there were also significant tax advantages to making inter vivos gifts rather than making gifts by will, but since the estate and gift tax rates are now unified, there are few remaining tax advantages. One remaining advantage to making an inter vivos gift is that if the gift appreciates in value between the time the gift is made and death, the appreciated value will not be subject to estate tax. If the gift were made by will, the added value would be taxable, since the gift would be valued on the estate tax return as of the date of death (or six months after).

IN PLAIN ENGLISH

This difference in value can represent significant tax savings for the heirs of someone whose business suddenly becomes successful and rapidly increases in value.

Annual Exclusion

The other advantage to making an inter vivos gift involves the yearly exclusion. A yearly exclusion of $12,000 per recipient is available on inter vivos gifts (other than gifts of future interests in property). For example, if $15,000 worth of gifts were given to an individual in one year, only $3,000 of its value will actually be taxable to the donor, who is responsible for the gift tax. A married couple can combine their gifts and claim a yearly exclusion of $24,000 per recipient, though each can gift only $12,000 tax-free. Note that the gift tax exemption is subject to change, and, while it is in effect in 2008, it is likely to increase. You should, therefore, check with your accountant to determine what the actual amount of the exemption is on the date the gift is made. In addition, there is an exclusion for gifts (other than gifts of future interest in property) to a spouse who is not a U.S. citizen. For 2008, that exclusion is $128,000.

Three-Year Rule

Gifts made within three years of death used to be included in the gross estate on the theory that they were made in contemplation of death. Amendments to the tax laws, however, have done away with the *three-year rule* for most purposes. The three-year rule is still applicable to gifts of life insurance and to certain transfers involving stock redemption or tax liens. The rule also applies to certain valuation schemes, the details of which are too complex to discuss here.

Gift Tax Returns

The donor must file a gift tax return for any year in which gifts made exceeded $12,000 to any one donee. It is not necessary to file a return when a gift to any one donee amounts to less than $12,000. However, where it is possible that valuation of the gift will become an issue with the IRS, it may be a good idea to file a return anyway. Filing the return starts the three-year statute of limitations running. Once the statute of limitations period has expired, the IRS will be barred from filing suit for unpaid taxes or for tax deficiencies due to higher government valuations of the gifts. If a taxpayer omits includable gifts amounting to more than 25% of the total amount of gifts stated in the return, the statute of limitations is extended to six years. There is no statute of limitations for fraudulent returns filed with the intent to evade tax.

In order to qualify as an inter vivos gift for tax purposes, a gift must be complete and final. Control is an important issue. If a giver retains the right to revoke a gift, the gift may be found to be testamentary in nature, even if the right to revoke was never exercised (unless the gift was made in trust). The gift must also be delivered. An actual, physical delivery is best, but a *symbolic delivery* may suffice if there is strong evidence of intent to make an irrevocable gift. An example of symbolic delivery is when the donor puts something in a safe and gives the intended recipient the only key.

Trusts

Another common way to transfer property outside the will is to place the property in a trust that is created prior to death. A *trust* is simply a legal arrangement by which one person holds certain property for the benefit of another. The person holding the property is the *trustee*. The trustee can be an individual or an institution, and in some situations, it may be beneficial to have more than one trustee. Those for whose benefit the trust is held are the *beneficiaries*. To create a valid trust, the giver must identify the trust property, make a declaration of intent to create the trust, transfer property to the trust, and name identifiable beneficiaries. If no trustee is named, a court will appoint one. The *settlor* (creator of the trust) may also be designated as trustee, in which case segregation of the trust property satisfies the delivery requirement. Trusts can be created by a will, in which case they are termed *testamentary trusts*, but these trust properties will be probated along with the rest of the will. To avoid probate, the settlor must create a valid inter vivos trust.

Inter Vivos Trusts

Generally, in order to qualify as an *inter vivos trust*, a valid interest in property must be transferred before the death of the creator of the trust. If the settlor fails to name a beneficiary for the trust or to make delivery of the property to the trustee before death, the trust will likely be termed testamentary. Such a trust will be deemed invalid unless the formalities required for creating a will were complied with.

A trust will not be termed *testamentary* simply because the settlor retained significant control over the trust, such as the power to revoke or modify the trust. For example, when a person makes a deposit in a savings account in his or her own name as trustee for another and reserves the power to withdraw the money or to revoke the trust, the trust will be enforceable by the beneficiary upon the death of the depositor, providing the depositor has not, in fact, revoked the trust.

IN PLAIN ENGLISH

Many states allow joint bank accounts with rights of survivorship to serve as valid will substitutes.

As Part of the Gross Estate

Property transferred and passed outside the will need not go through probate. However, even though such an arrangement escapes probate, the trust property will probably be counted as part of the gross estate for tax purposes because the settlor retained significant control. In addition, if the deceased settlor created a revocable trust for the purpose of decreasing the share of a surviving spouse, in some states the trust will be declared illusory—in effect, invalid. The surviving spouse is then granted the legal share from the probated estate and from the revocable trust.

Life Insurance Trusts

Life insurance trusts can be used for paying estate taxes. The proceeds will not be taxed if the life insurance trust is irrevocable and the beneficiary is someone other than the estate, such as a friend or relative in an individual capacity or a business. This is especially important for businesspeople, since, without a life insurance trust, their survivors might be forced to sell estate assets for less than their real value in order to pay estate taxes.

PROBATE

Briefly described, *probate* is the legal process by which a decedent's estate is administered in a systematic and orderly manner and with finality. The laws that govern the probate process vary among states. One of the principal functions of probate administration is to provide a means to transfer ownership of a decedent's probate property. Accordingly, probate administration occurs without regard to whether the decedent died testate or intestate.

In the course of probate administration, the following occurs.

- A decedent's will is admitted to probate as the decedent's last will.

- A personal representative, executor, or administrator is appointed by the court to take charge of the decedent's property and financial affairs.

- Interested persons are notified of the commencement of probate administration.

- Information concerning the decedent's estate is gathered.

- Probate property is assembled and preserved.

- Debts and taxes are determined, paid, or challenged.

- Claims against the decedent's estate are paid or challenged.

- Conflicting claims of entitlement to the decedent's property are disposed of.

- At the conclusion of the process, the remaining estate property is distributed to the appropriate persons or entities.

While probate administration is pending, distributions of the decedent's property are suspended to allow creditors, claimants, devisees, and heirs the opportunity to protect their respective rights.

Probate property consists of the decedent's solely owned property as of the date of death. Property jointly held by the decedent and another person with the right of survivorship (i.e., a residence or stock certificates owned jointly with right of survivorship) passes to the survivor and is not a part of the decedent's probate estate. Likewise, the proceeds of life insurance on the decedent's life are not part of the probate estate (unless the estate is the designated beneficiary). It is, therefore, possible for a wealthy individual to die leaving little or no probate property.

CHAPTER 17

Finding a Lawyer and an Accountant

Most health care professionals expect to seek the advice of a lawyer only occasionally, for counseling on important matters such as the decision to incorporate or the purchase of a building. If this is your concept of the attorney's role in your business, you need to reevaluate it. Most health care practices would operate more efficiently and more profitably in the long run if they had a relationship with a business attorney more like that between a family doctor and patient. An ongoing relationship that allows the attorney to get to know the practice well enough to engage in preventive legal counseling and to assist in planning makes it possible to solve many problems before they occur.

If your practice is small or undercapitalized, you are undoubtedly anxious to keep operating costs down. You probably do not relish the idea of paying an attorney to get to know your practice if you are not involved in an immediate crisis. However, it is a good bet that a visit with a competent business lawyer right now will result in the raising of issues vital to the future of your practice. There is good reason why larger, successful businesses employ one or more attorneys full-time as in-house counsel. Ready access to legal advice is something you should not deny your practice at any time, for any reason.

An experienced attorney can give you important information regarding the risks unique to your practice. Furthermore, a lawyer can advise you regarding your rights and obligations in your relationship with present and future employees, the rules that apply in your state regarding the hiring and firing of employees, permissible collection practices, and so forth. Ignorance of these issues and violation of the rules can result in financially devastating lawsuits and even criminal penalties. Since each state has its own laws covering certain business practices, state laws must be consulted on many areas covered in this book. A competent local business attorney is, therefore, your best source of information on many issues that will arise in the operation of your business. Many law firms have attorneys who are licensed in several jurisdictions, and others have relationships with attorneys in other locales.

IN PLAIN ENGLISH

Most legal problems cost more to solve after they arise than it would have cost to prevent their occurrence in the first place. Litigation is notoriously inefficient and expensive. You do not want to sue or to be sued, if you can help it.

FINDING A LAWYER

If you do not know any attorneys, ask other health care practitioners or businesspeople if they know any good ones. You want either a lawyer who specializes in business or a general practitioner who has many satisfied business clients. You may even be able to find an attorney who specializes in representing health care practices and related businesses. Finding the lawyer who is right for you may require that you shop around a bit. Most local and state bar associations have referral services. A good tip is to find out who is in the business law section of the state or local bar association or who has served on special bar committees dealing with law reform. It may also be useful to find out if any articles covering the area of law with which you are concerned have been published in either scholarly journals or continuing-legal-education publications and if the author is available to assist you.

It is a good idea to hire a specialist or law firm with a number of specialists rather than a general practitioner. While it is true that you may pay more per hour for the expert, you will not have to pay for the attorney's learning time. Experience is valuable. In this regard, you may wish to keep in mind that it is uncommon for a lawyer to specialize in business practice and also handle criminal matters. Thus, if you are faced with a criminal prosecution for the death of an employee, you should be searching for an experienced criminal defense lawyer.

Evaluating a Lawyer

You may wish to search the Internet for information on attorneys, since many law firms have established websites. The larger firms usually include extensive information about themselves, their practice areas, and their attorneys. Another method by which you can attempt to evaluate an attorney in regard to representing business clients is by consulting one of the law directories, such as **www.martindale.com**. However, the mere fact that an attorney's name does not appear in a given directory should not be given much weight, since there is an extraordinarily high charge for being included and many lawyers have chosen not to pay for the listings.

After you have obtained several recommendations for attorneys, it is appropriate for you to talk with them for a short period of time to determine whether you would be comfortable working with them. Do not be afraid to ask about their background, experience, and whether they feel they can help you.

Using a Lawyer

Once you have completed the interview process, select the person who appears to best satisfy your needs. One of the first items you should discuss with your lawyer is the fee structure. You are entitled to an estimate. However, unless you enter into an agreement to the contrary with the attorney, the estimate is just that. Business lawyers generally charge by the hour, though you may be quoted a flat rate for a specific service, such as incorporation or a simple will.

Contact your lawyer whenever you believe a legal question has arisen. Your attorney should aid you in identifying which questions require legal action or advice and which require business decisions. Generally, lawyers will deal only with legal issues, though they may help you to evaluate business problems.

Some attorneys encourage clients to feel comfortable calling at the office during the day or at home in the evening. Other lawyers, however, may resent having their personal time invaded. Some, in fact, do not list their home telephone numbers. You should learn your attorney's preference early on.

The attorney-client relationship is such that you should feel comfortable when confiding in your attorney. This person will not disclose your confidential communications; in fact, a violation of this rule, depending on the circumstances, can be considered an ethical breach that could subject the attorney to professional sanctions.

If you take the time to develop a good working relationship with your attorney, it may well prove to be one of your more valuable business assets.

FINDING AN ACCOUNTANT

In addition to an attorney, most small businesses will need the services of a competent accountant to aid with tax planning, the filing of periodic reports, and annual tax returns. Finding an accountant with whom your business is compatible is similar to finding an attorney. You should ask around and learn which accountants are servicing businesses similar to yours. State professional accounting associations may also provide a referral service or point you to a directory of accountants in your area. You should interview prospective accountants to determine whether you feel you can work with them and whether you feel their skills will be compatible with your business needs.

Like your attorney, your accountant can provide valuable assistance in planning for the future of your business. It is important to work with professionals you trust and with whom you are able to relate on a professional level.

Glossary

A

action. A lawsuit filed with a court.

administrator. The person appointed by a probate court to administer the estate of someone who has died. Also known as a personal representative or executor/executrix.

admissible. Evidence that can be properly presented in court and considered by the judge or jury.

advance directive. A health care power of attorney and/or instructions about the kind of care one would like to have if he or she becomes unable to make medical decisions.

affidavit. A notarized, written statement about facts, made under penalty of perjury. *See also* declaration, notary public.

agent. A person who is authorized to carry out activities on behalf of another, known as a principal, and to enter into agreements that bind the principal.

alternative dispute resolution (ADR). A process of settling a dispute without the necessity of a formal lawsuit or trial; includes arbitration, mediation, and settlement.

answer. The pleading by which a defendant responds to the plaintiff's allegation of facts, technically known as a *complaint*.

appeal. A proceeding in which a higher court or tribunal reviews the decision of a lower court, agency, or arbitration award. *See also* appellant, appellate court, appellee.

appellant. The party who has appealed a decision or judgment to a higher court or tribunal. Also known as an appellant-petitioner. *See also* appeal, appellate court, appellee.

appellate court. A court or tribunal having jurisdiction to review the judgments of a lower court, agency, or arbitration award. *See also* appeal, appellant, appellee.

appellee. The party against whom an appeal is filed. Also known as an appellee-respondent. *See also* appeal, appellant, appellate court.

arbitration. A mandatory or voluntary proceeding to resolve a dispute conducted outside the courts by one or more independent third parties selected by the parties to the dispute. Arbitration awards may or may not be final or appealable. *See also* alternative dispute resolution, appeal, mediation.

articles of incorporation. A document filed with a state in order to formally create a corporation's legal existence. *See also* board of directors, corporation, officers.

articles of organization. A document filed with a state in order to formally create a limited liability company's legal existence. *See also* limited liability company.

assignment. A transfer of an asset or right by its owner to another.

B

bad faith. Dishonesty or deceit in a transaction, such as entering into an agreement with no intention of performing according to its terms. *See also* good faith.

bailment. A relationship created when one's property is in the rightful possession of another; e.g., an X-ray machine sent to a shop for repair. The custodian of the property (shop) is known as a bailee; the owner of the property (practitioner) is a bailor.

balance sheet. A financial report that shows assets over liabilities. It shows the financial situation of the business at the time the financial statement was compiled.

bankruptcy. Judicial proceedings in which persons or businesses that are legally insolvent may satisfy creditors or discharge debts.

beneficiary. The person or entity designated to receive a benefit through a formal instrument such as a will, trust, insurance policy, or the like. *See also* grantee.

bequeath. To give money to another through a will. *See also* bequest.

bequest. The money or property given through a will. *See also* bequeath.

board of directors. The group charged by state law and elected by a corporation's shareholders to run the business and affairs of a corporation. *See also* corporation, officers.

breach of contract. Failure to perform a contractual obligation.

burden of proof. The obligation of the party bringing a lawsuit to prove its case. Generally, in criminal cases, the state must prove its case beyond a reasonable doubt; in civil cases, the plaintiff must prove its case by a preponderance of evidence; in a case of fraud, proof must be demonstrated by clear and convincing evidence. *See also* clear and convincing evidence, preponderance of evidence, reasonable doubt.

business interruption insurance. Insurance covering lost profits in the event your location is unusable.

bylaws. A corporation's internal rules and regulations.

C

capital gain. The profit made from the sale of a capital asset such as real estate, stocks, and bonds.

capital loss. The loss that results from the sale of a capital asset such as real estate, stocks, and bonds.

case law. Law based on judicial decisions.

cause of action. A lawsuit.

caveat emptor. "Let the buyer beware"; the doctrine that a buyer assumes the risks of purchase.

charitable trust. A trust set up to fulfill a charitable mission.

citation. In legal reference, a means for identifying a case, administrative proceeding, rule, statute, and the like.

civil action. A noncriminal lawsuit. A lawsuit filed by a person or company to redress a wrong (*tort*) or to obtain a benefit (*contract*). Differs from a criminal action, brought by a government (local, state, or federal) for violation of a penal statute (felony or misdemeanor).

claim. An assertion of a right to money, property, or some other benefit or forbearance.

clear and convincing evidence. The standard of proof requiring the truth of the facts asserted to be highly probable. *See also* burden of proof, preponderance of evidence, reasonable doubt.

codicil. An addition to a will.

common law. Law arising from tradition and judicial decisions rather than laws, rules, and regulations. *See also* stare decisis.

comparative advertising. A form of advertising in which one's goods or services are compared to those of another. Such advertising is regulated and must not be misleading.

complaint. The initial document filed in court by a party making a claim. *See also* answer.

condition. A circumstance imposed or agreed to by the parties to a contract before or after which performance or forbearance must occur. *See also* forbearance, performance.

confidentiality agreement. An agreement whereby one or more parties to the agreement agree not to use or disclose certain confidential information, except as expressly permitted by that agreement.

consent. Agreement.

conservator. A person with the legal right and obligation to manage the property and financial affairs of another. *See also* guardian.

consideration. Something of value given in return for something else of equivalent value, including money, property, performance, or forbearance. *See also* forbearance, performance.

contract. A legally enforceable agreement between two or more parties.

copyright. The right to publish, distribute, reproduce, perform, or display a work or to exclude others from doing the same.

corporation. A hypothetical legal person created by statute for the purpose of engaging in lawful activity. It may be for commercial purposes (a business or professional corporation) or for charitable purposes (nonprofit corporation). *See also* articles of incorporation, board of directors, officers.

counterclaim. A claim by a defendant in a civil case against the plaintiff.

court costs. The fees assessed by a court for use of its resources in connection with a court proceeding.

D

damages. Monetary compensation that may be recovered in the courts by any person who has suffered loss, detriment, or injury to his or her person, property, or rights through the unlawful act or negligence of another.

declaration. A written statement about facts, made under penalty of perjury. Unlike affidavits, declarations are typically not notarized.

defamation. The act of injuring a person's reputation. *See also* libel, slander.

defendant. The person or entity against whom a lawsuit is brought. *See also* plaintiff.

donor. A person or entity that gives money or property to another; e.g., one who makes donations to charity.

due process. Technically, "fair process." The regular course of administration of law through the courts or administrative bodies.

duress. Conduct that attempts to compel a person to do something he or she otherwise would not do.

duty to warn. The legal obligation to warn of a potential danger.

E

elective share. The right of a spouse under probate law to take a specified portion of an estate when the other spouse dies, regardless of what was stated in the will.

employee. A person hired by another, who does not provide the services as part of an independent business. *See also* independent contractor.

enjoin. A court's action through the issuance of an order to require a person to perform or to abstain from a specific act. *See also* injunction.

equitable action. An action brought to restrain a wrongful act or prevent a threatened illegal action.

escheat. The process by which a deceased person's property goes to the state if no heir can be located.

estate. A person or entity's personal property, real property, and intangible property.

estate tax. A tax assessed against the taxable assets of an estate. *See also* estate.

executor/executrix. The person appointed by a probate court to administer the estate of someone who has died. Also known as an administrator or personal representative.

express warranty. An explicit promise or statement concerning the quality of goods or services.

F

federal law. Federal statutes, regulations, and court rulings.

fiduciary. A person having a legal relationship of trust and confidence with another and having a duty to act primarily for the other person's benefit; for example, a guardian, trustee, or executor.

forbearance. The agreement or obligation of a party not to take an action. *See also* performance.

fraud. An intentional act designed to induce or deprive another person through deception.

G

general partner. A partner who has the right and obligation to participate in the management of a partnership and who has unlimited personal liability for its debts. *See also* limited partner, limited partnership.

good faith. Honesty in a transaction, such as entering into an agreement with every intention of performing according to its terms. *See also* bad faith.

Good Samaritan laws. Laws protecting those who provide good faith medical aid in an emergency from liability. Such laws vary from state to state.

grantee. A person who receives property from another, either outright or through a trust. *See also* beneficiary, grantor.

grantor. The person who gives property to another, either outright or through a trust. Also known as a settlor or trustor. *See also* grantee.

guardian. A person appointed by the court to be responsible for the care and management of affairs for another, generally an incompetent adult or minor child. *See also* conservator.

H

hearsay. A statement by a person who did not have firsthand knowledge of the content of the statement. Hearsay is generally inadmissible in court.

holographic will. A handwritten will.

hospital privileges. Permission to use a hospital's facilities in connection with one's health care practice.

I

implied contract. Not explicitly written or stated; determined by deduction from known facts or from the circumstances or conduct of the parties.

implied warranty. A guarantee imposed by law even in the absence of an explicit promise.

income statement. A financial statement that reflects profits and losses by showing earnings minus expenses over a period of time. It shows whether the business incurred a profit or loss during the given period.

income tax. A tax levied on income or receipts.

incompetent. Unable to make or carry out important decisions.

independent contractor. A person or business that performs services for others but is not subject to the other's direct control. *See also* employee.

infringement. The violation of another's intellectual property right such as a copyright, trademark, or patent.

inheritance tax. A state tax levied on an heir or beneficiary for property received under a will.

injunction. An order of the court prohibiting or compelling the performance or forbearance of a specific act. *See also* enjoin, forbearance, performance.

intangible assets. Items such as intellectual property or other rights that do not have physical manifestation but nevertheless have value.

intellectual property. A form of creative expression that can be protected through copyright, trade dress, trademark, trade secret, patent, and the like.

inter vivos gift. A gift made during the donor's lifetime.

inter vivos trust. A trust created during the trustor's lifetime. *See also* living trust, testamentary trust.

intestate. Dying without a will.

intestate succession. The order of distribution of the property of a person who has died without a will. The order of distribution varies from state to state.

irrevocable trust. A trust that may not be revoked by the trustor.

J

joint tenancy. A form of property ownership in which two or more surviving parties own undivided interests in property and where the co-owner becomes the sole owner of the property after the other co-owner dies.

judgment. The final disposition of a lawsuit.

jurisdiction. A court's ability to hear a case brought before it.

just cause. A legitimate and lawful reason for taking a particular action.

L

liable. Legally responsible.

libel. A form of defamation expressed in the form of written words or graphic images. *See also* slander.

license. A legal right or permission; e.g., a driver's license or a license to practice one's profession.

lien. A claim against another person's property. Liens may be created by common law, statute, or contract. For example, a mechanic's lien is given for payment of work performed on another's property.

limited liability company. A hypothetical legal person created by statute for the purpose of conducting business.

limited partner. A partner who provides financial backing to a limited partnership but whose liability for partnership debts is limited to its investment. *See also* general partner.

limited partnership. A partnership with one or more general partners and one or more limited partners.

litigant. A party in a lawsuit.

living trust. A trust created during the lifetime of the grantor. Also known as an *inter vivos trust.*

M

malpractice. Negligence in the treatment of a patient; failure to provide the quality of care that is reasonably expected in the circumstances.

mediation. A form of alternative dispute resolution in which the parties voluntarily bring their dispute to a neutral third party who helps them reach a voluntary settlement. *See also* arbitration.

minor. A person who does not have the legal rights of an adult, generally under the age of 18.

N

negligence. Acting or failing to act in accordance with the standards established for a reasonable person in the particular locale.

notary public. Any person commissioned by the state to perform notarial acts as defined by law. *See also* affidavit.

O

obligation. The requirement to do or refrain from doing what is imposed by a law, promise, contract, or court order.

offer. An act expressing willingness to enter into a contract.

officers. The people charged with the day-to-day responsibility for running a corporation, such as the president and chief financial officer. *See also* board of directors, bylaws, corporation.

operating agreement. A limited liability company's internal rules and regulations.

opinion. A written decision of a court that explains the rationale behind the decision.

option. A type of contract that gives the holder the right to buy or sell a specific property at a fixed price for a limited period of time; also any choice.

P

partnership. An association of two or more persons who are engaged in a business for profit.

party. A person named in a contract or legal proceeding. Plaintiffs and defendants are parties to initial lawsuits; appellants and appellees are parties in appeals.

performance. The taking of an action. *See also* forbearance.

perjury. The criminal offense of making a false statement under oath.

personal property. Tangible physical property and intangible assets that are not land or rights in land.

personal representative. The person appointed by a probate court to administer the estate of someone who has died. Also known as an administrator or executor/executrix. *See also* estate.

plaintiff. The person who files a complaint in a civil lawsuit. *See also* defendant.

precedent. A previously decided case or course of conduct that guides future decisions. *See also* stare decisis.

preponderance of evidence. A standard of proof requiring the weight of the evidence to make a particular finding more probable than improbable.

presumption. A rule of law establishing that a particular hypothesis is true unless evidence to the contrary is presented to rebut it; e.g., a criminal defendant is presumed innocent until proven guilty.

principal. The person whom an agent serves and who may be legally bound by the agent.

probate court. The court with the authority and obligation to supervise estate administration.

probate estate. Estate property that may be disposed of by a will.

professional corporation. A business form available to professionals that offers some, but not all, of the benefits of limited liability enjoyed by a business corporation.

professional liability insurance. Covers liability resulting from a practitioner's negligent treatment of a patient. *See also* malpractice.

property right. The right to use or possess a determinate thing.

R

real property. Land, buildings, and the improvements thereon.

reasonable care. The level of care an ordinary person would use under specific circumstances.

reasonable doubt. A standard of proof where uncertainty is created in the mind of the person considering the evidence. *See also* clear and convincing evidence, preponderance of the evidence.

receiver. A person appointed by a court or government agency to manage the property of another. *See also* guardian.

S

security interest. A legal term for a lender's rights in collateral.

settlor. *See* grantor.

slander. A form of defamation expressed orally. *See also* libel.

small claims court. A proceeding for disputes over small amounts, usually $5,000–$10,000, depending on the state.

sole proprietorship. The method of conducting business by an individual who has full personal liability for all acts and contracts of the business.

specific performance. The requirement of a person (made by a court) to perform specifically what he or she originally agreed to do.

staff privileges. Permission to use a hospital's facilities in connection with one's health care practice.

standing. The legal right to sue or pursue a claim on a particular matter.

stare decisis. The doctrine that courts will adhere to the principles established in prior cases.

state law. Statutes, regulations, and rulings having the force of law.

statute of frauds. A body of laws requiring certain transactions to be evidenced by a writing to be enforceable.

statute of limitations. Sometimes referred to as statute of repose, a law setting the time period within which a lawsuit must be filed. It is intended to balance the rights of the parties by providing a limited period within which rights may be enforced and wrongs redressed. After the period expires, the other party may claim the statute as a defense to the action.

statutes. Laws enacted by legislatures.

stay. An order suspending a judicial proceeding.

subpoena. A court order compelling a witness's attendance.

subpoena duces tecum. A court order that requires a witness to produce certain documents or records.

substantive law. Law dealing with the rights, duties, and liabilities of people, as opposed to law that regulates procedures followed by courts and agencies.

suit in equity. *See* equitable action.

summary judgment. A court order issued in a lawsuit because there is no triable issue of fact.

T

testamentary capacity. The legal ability to make a will.

testamentary trust. A trust set up pursuant to a will. *See also* inter vivos trust, living trust.

testimony. Spoken evidence given under oath.

third-party claim. A claim filed by a defendant that brings a previously unnamed third party into an existing lawsuit. *See also* counterclaim.

title. Legal ownership of or to property.

tort. A civil wrong.

trademark. A word, symbol, logo, or design used to distinguish the goods and services of one person or organization from others in the marketplace.

trust. A legal instrument used to manage property, established by one person for the benefit of him- or herself or another. *See also* inter vivos trust, living trust, testamentary trust.

trustee. A person who manages property held in trust. *See also* grantor, settlor, trustor.

trustor. *See* grantor.

V

venue. The particular court in which a case is to be tried.

verdict. The decision rendered by a jury.

vicarious liability. Indirect liability for the actions of another.

W

waive. To voluntarily give up a right or claim.

warranty. A kind of contract with respect to property. For example, a deed for the sale of land can be a full covenant and warranty deed, or a warranty may be granted when personal property is sold.

will. The legal declaration that governs the disposition of a person's property when that person dies. Also known as a last will and testament.

Index

About the Authors

Leonard D. DuBoff is an internationally recognized expert who has lectured on legal issues around the world. He began his legal career in New York, and then relocated to Palo Alto, California, where he started teaching at the Stanford Law School. Subsequently, he moved to Portland, Oregon, where he taught law at Lewis & Clark Law School. DuBoff spent almost a quarter of a century teaching business and intellectual property law.

While a full-time law professor, DuBoff was also of counsel to law firms and maintained that relationship until 1994, when he left full-time teaching to found his own law firm that specializes in business and intellectual property law. DuBoff has received academic awards from President Lyndon Johnson and New York Governor Nelson Rockefeller, and in 1990, he received the Governor's Arts Award from Oregon Governor Neil Goldschmidt.

A prolific author, DuBoff has written numerous articles for scholarly journals, practical articles for lawyers' bar publications, and articles for nonlawyers, as well. DuBoff continues to serve as an educator by presenting continuing legal education programs for attorneys and seminars for nonlawyers.

Christy O. King is an attorney in Portland, Oregon, where she is a principal with The DuBoff Law Group, LLC. She is licensed to practice in Oregon and Washington and for 15 years has had an active practice representing clients in intellectual property, business, employment, contract, and corporate law matters. She is coauthor of four other books, as well as of numerous scholarly and practical articles. King earned her law degree cum laude from Lewis & Clark Law School.

Michael D. Murray obtained his law degree from Columbia Law School, where he was a Harlan Fiske Stone Scholar. After law school, he clerked for United States District Judge John F. Nangle of the Eastern District of Missouri. He also practiced commercial, intellectual property, and products liability litigation for several years in St. Louis. Since 2002, he has been a professor at the University of Illinois College of Law. He is the author or coauthor of fourteen books on topics ranging from advocacy, art law, civil procedure, First Amendment, and freedom of expression, to legal research and legal writing, and products liability law.